Design Essentials

Design Essentials
A HANDBOOK

Jonathan Block
Gisele Atterberry
Parkland College, Champaign, Illinois

PRENTICE HALL Englewood Cliffs, NJ 07632

Library of Congress Cataloging-in-Publication Data

Block, Jonathan
  Design essentials.

  Includes index.
  1. Design--Handbooks, manuals, etc. I. Atterberry,
Gisele. II. Title.
NK1510.B578 1988   745.4   88-23181
ISBN 0-13-200155-1

Editorial/production supervision and
   interior design: Arthur Maisel
Cover design: Photo Plus Art
Line Drawings: Elizabeth Fathauer
Manufacturing buyer: Ray Keating
Page layout: Gail Cocker

© 1989 by Prentice-Hall, Inc.
A Division of Simon & Schuster
Englewood Cliffs, New Jersey 07632

Printed in the United States of America

10 9 8 7 6 5 4 3 2 1

ISBN 0-13-200155-1

Prentice-Hall International (UK) Limited, *London*
Prentice-Hall of Australia Pty. Limited, *Sydney*
Prentice-Hall Canada Inc., *Toronto*
Prentice-Hall Hispanoamericana, S.A., *Mexico*
Prentice-Hall of India Private Limited, *New Delhi*
Prentice-Hall of Japan, Inc., *Tokyo*
Simon & Schuster Asia Pte. Ltd., *Singapore*
Editora Prentice-Hall do Brasil, Ltda., *Rio de Janeiro*

Contents

Preface   vii

Acknowledgments   ix

1   The Design Process   1

      Originality and sources   2
      The creative process   3
      Art and athletics: An analogy   8
      About college   9

2   The Glossary   10

3   Exercises and Analysis   153

      Exercises   153
      Analysis: Twenty questions   155
      Critiques: Strategies and questions   156

Index of Artists' Names   159

Preface

Two-Dimensional Design, along with Beginning Drawing and Art History Survey, forms the foundation of most contemporary training in the visual arts. We seek in our courses to provide students with basic tools that will enable them to make the most of their continuing education in art and be of value to them regardless of their ultimate careers. Therefore, the focus in our courses is on conceptual tools, rather than mechanical skills. Moreover, we seek to develop our students' awareness of the basic issues that they will be confronting throughout their creative lives and to equip them to deal productively with the challenges that they will surely encounter.

In developing *Design Essentials*, we have sought to create a tool which will be useful to our students, as well as to our colleagues (and ourselves) in teaching. There are many traditional texts organized around the elements and principles of design, but often we found ourselves presenting information in terms of conceptual or thematic issues. Frustrated by the necessarily linear and hierarchical presentation of material in more traditional texts, we sought a new organizational structure—but we soon realized that we were merely creating an alternative hierarchy. It was still a confining rather than a liberating structure.

At this point it occurred to us that what we really needed was simply a *glossary*. While the structure, order, and form of our courses has varied enormously over the years, the central content remains the same; we continue to develop the same range of awarenesses and skills in our students. What changes is our emphasis and methods of presentation. The alphabetical structure of a glossary allows us to put the essential information at our fingertips without imposing a specific conceptual structure upon us or our students.

In selecting illustrations for the text we have limited

ourselves to modern and contemporary images. The text is intentionally not historical in its organization or presentation. While we believe deeply in the value of history as a source and a resource, design as the core of studio foundations is a contemporary idea: We feel it is best taught through the medium of contemporary images and ideas.

The text is designed to serve as a handbook that supports the teaching of instructors and programs with evolving or well-developed curricula. We assume that the instructor will use the information provided to reinforce an existing curriculum. We ask our students to read parts 1 and 3 and to skim part 2, the glossary, at the beginning of the semester. The information in the glossary is regularly referred to in assigning problems and in critique. The shared references it provides, both verbal and visual, facilitate effective communication among all members of the class.

The glossary contains three general types of terms: those describing visual elements or design principles, those describing media or materials, and those describing critical ideas or historical styles and movements. We included the latter in order to support historical references in critique, and to encourage the students' awareness of modern and contemporary art as central parts of the cultural context within which they work.

Acknowledgments

There are many to whom I am indebted in the writing of this book. First, I would like to thank Bud Therien of Prentice Hall for taking seriously my suggestion that a glossary could provide the framework for an introductory design text. The project would not have begun without his support and encouragement. Equal thanks go to my co-author, Gisele. Her depth of knowledge, wit, and attention to detail are responsible for the thoroughness of the text. I owe special thanks to Elizabeth Fathauer, an ex-student and our illustrator, for developing outstanding illustrations with a minimum of guidance. Somehow she was able to read my mind. Professor Donald Lake of Parkland College reviewed the manuscript and brought many gaps in my knowledge to my attention. Finally, I thank my family, especially my wife, for their patience and support. They are the source of meaning in my life, and give purpose to my work.

Jonathan Block

It is a pleasure to note the assistance of those who aided in many different ways in the completion of this text. First of all, I am pleased to express my gratitude to my co-author, Jonathan Block. Jonathan developed the original concept for this book, and his sensitivity and intelligence shaped each page. I am indebted to him for inviting me to share in the project. One of the benefits of working with Jonathan was the opportunity to better know his wife, Kathy, who generously assisted us throughout the writing process. I would also like to acknowledge the help of our collegue Don

Lake, who offered much appreciated advice as we prepared the final manuscript, as well as the full cooperation of our graphic artist, Elizabeth Fathauer, who cheerfully shared in the proofreading. The guidance of our editor, Bud Therien, was essential. Arthur Maisel, our production editor, attended to a long list of details with utmost professionalism. Space limitations prohibit me from listing individually the many gallery and museum personnel who aided in compiling images for the text, but I deeply appreciate their invaluable contributions of time and effort. Finally, I would like to offer special thanks to my friends and family, especially my husband Richard and daughter Rachel, for their encouragement and support.

Gisele Atterberry

Design Essentials

A HANDBOOK

1

The Design Process

de · sign *verb* to plan; to scheme; to intend for a definite purpose; to conceive; to think out considering the consequences and the interrelationships of sequential events.

Design is an active process. When asked to form a picture in our minds of an artist or designer at work, we are inclined to visualize someone involved in painting, drawing, or sculpting. We think of the work of the artist or designer primarily as the manipulation of materials. In fact, a substantial amount of an artist's time is spent on the design process—thinking and looking. When confronted with a problem, an artist does not wait for inspiration, but rather applies the learned principles of design to develop appropriate strategies for meeting the visual challenge. When things are going well and ideas are flowing, this design activity may be carried out intuitively. When things get difficult, we call on our training.

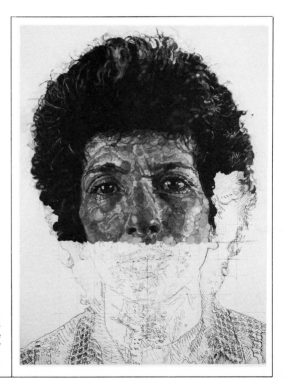

FIGURE 1 Chuck Close, *Phyllis*, 1984, pulp paper collage on canvas (work in progress) 8′ × 6′. Courtesy of The Pace Gallery, New York. Photo by Zindman/ Fremont.

The design process involves two major areas of challenge: generating ideas and realizing them. The first area is approached by developing skills of problem definition and ideation; the second by developing manual skills and abilities in analysis and judgment. In this section we will first consider sources for ideas, and then the creative process. Finally, we will compare the training of artists with the training of athletes and discuss the study of art in a college or university setting.

ORIGINALITY AND SOURCES

Beginning students sometimes feel that the greatest difficulty they face is generating ideas. This frustration can be the result of a limited understanding of the creative process and misconceptions about the idea of originality. Many bring to their creative work a false idea of the romantic muse and expect artists to be consumed with passion and somehow divinely or diabolically inspired. This misconception can result in a paralysis of "waiting for ideas," an artist's version of "writer's block." Artists and designers are visual problem solvers. They cannot just wait for inspiration; they must use their eyes and minds to look for ideas.

Designers and artists have the whole world as a source book. Our ideas spring from experiences and our interpretations of them. They arise from what we have seen, read, felt, and heard. Original ideas result from the forming of new relationships and connections, enabling us to see and relate to the world in new ways. To produce original ideas we must avail ourselves of the widest possible range of knowledge and experience.

There are many rich sources of ideas. Foremost among these sources is the work of other artists. Artists have always drawn ideas from the work of their contemporaries and those who preceded them (Figure 2). To deny yourself access to this vast resource is to attempt to work in a vacuum. When contemporary artists are asked to name those whose work has had a great influence on them, they often mention the "old masters." Even the most radical work of today is firmly rooted in the past. Libraries are readily accessible and, with their collections of art periodicals and books, can be as valuable a source of ideas and inspiration as museums and galleries.

Have you ever looked at someone else's work and said to yourself "I wish that idea were mine"? It can be. Just because someone else has expressed an idea, you are not precluded from pursuing the same idea, imbuing it with uniqueness in the specific ways in which you present it. If you see an idea you wish were your own in the work of another, you should feel free to take it. In developing it, you will make it your own. This is not copying or plagiarism, rather it is in the highest tradition of artistic growth and development.

If you wish to understand the ways in which forms can be combined, you need only to actively look at and observe the world around you. Eyes can function as much more than radar to keep you from walking into walls. Vision need not be passive. It can be active, interpretive, and challenging.

For many, a most important resource is their fellow artists. Other artists are able to look at our work from a different perspective, making us more aware of the effect that the work communicates. They can help us to recognize

FIGURE 2 Hans van Hoek, *"Studie van Rubens" Venus tracht Mars in te houden (De Gevolgen van de Oorlog* ["Study After Rubens" Venus Attempts to Hold Mars (The Consequences of War)], 1986, oil on canvas, 66½ × 118⅞". Courtesy of Irene Hochman.

potential problems and offer possible solutions. All too often, we do not gain valuable insights until critique time. Through discussion with others, these insights could have come much sooner. Do not wait until a critique to seek responses to your work. Ask your fellow students for their comments. Communication with your colleagues should be an ongoing process.

THE CREATIVE PROCESS

While it is true that new ideas sometimes seem to leap unbidden to the front of our consciousness, most often they result from a careful and thoughtful analysis of the problem at hand. Creative persons in all fields are interested in the methodology of creativity, and many models of the creative process have been put forward. One of the simplest

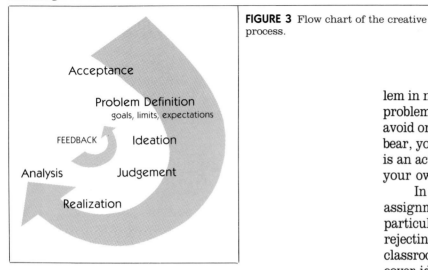

FIGURE 3 Flow chart of the creative process.

and most useful (Figure 3) divides the process into several steps: acceptance, problem definition, ideation, judgment, realization, and analysis.

Two items are important to note in this model. One is that ideation, the generation of ideas, does not come first. The second is that ideation is separate from judgment. If you can keep these two things in mind, you are well on your way to becoming an effective problem solver.

Acceptance

The first step in any creative problem-solving situation is to consciously *accept* the problem. This may seem unnecessary, but occasionally you may find yourself in the middle of a problem without ever having decided that you really want to solve it or without believing that it really is a prob-

lem in need of solution. Lacking any real desire to solve the problem, you direct your creative energies toward efforts to avoid or eliminate it. If you want to bring your creativity to bear, you must *want* to solve the problem. What is required is an active receptivity, a willingness to "make the problem your own."

In class situations you may be confronted with an assignment which seems to be of little relevance to your particular interests or goals. Rather than resisting or rejecting the problem, keep in mind the unique goals of the classroom situation. The class offers an opportunity to discover ideas, materials, or approaches that you might have been reluctant or unlikely to explore in other circumstances.

Mature artists often focus their attention on a narrow area of concerns, exploring in depth a limited problem. If you look at a survey of the life work of an artist, you are likely to be struck not by the variety in his or her work, but by its unity. As a beginning student, however, you should expose yourself to the greatest variety of experiences and attitudes. It is at this stage of your growth that you build the visual and experiential vocabulary that you will draw from for the rest of your life. If you limit yourself now, you will have less at your disposal in the years to come. Be willing to approach problems with an open mind. While your assignments may not seem relevant to your immediate personal interests, your responses to them will provide valuable experiences.

Problem Definition

Accepting a problem is closely tied to defining it. To accept a problem, you must first understand what the problem is. *Problem definition* involves attempting to spell out as clearly as possible what you want to accomplish, taking care to make no false or unnecessary assumptions. Problem definition is the process of defining goals and establishing limits. Your definition of a problem determines the areas in which you will seek and find solutions.

Before beginning on a project, it may be useful to ask the following questions:

- What are the goals of this project; what is it intended to accomplish?
- What are my goals; what do I hope to achieve through this project?
- What are the instructor's expectations?
- What are the project's limits in terms of scale, materials, methods of execution, presentation, time, and so on?
- Can I restate the problem in such a way that it incorporates all of these goals and limitations—the instructor's and my own?

At this point you are ready to proceed, keeping in mind that it is always possible, and often desirable, to return to this stage of the creative process. As your work proceeds, your understanding of the problem is likely to change. This evolving understanding of the issues can result in a need to redefine the problem and reaffirm your acceptance of the challenge.

Only after honestly accepting and carefully defining the problem should you attempt to proceed. Many creative failures result from either a refusal to accept the problem or an improper understanding of it.

Ideation

This is the part of the process that is usually associated with intellectual creativity. At this point you come up with ideas and possible solutions to the problem. Your goal should be to *generate as many different ideas as possible* without screening them into categories of "good" or "bad."

The most common mistake is to judge your ideas immediately, before taking time to explore them. An idea comes to mind and it is rejected as inappropriate, or you decide that it is too difficult or that it will not work. First ideas, because they are "obvious," come to mind immediately, often flowing into the sketchbook before you fully comprehend the problem. They are frequently followed by less promising possibilities. It is important to suspend judgment and record these ideas as well.

Sketching is the primary tool for this brainstorming. Not only does it create a record of your thought process, but also, the physical act of sketching, coupled with the visual involvement in looking at what you draw, acts as a springboard for new ideas. One sketch leads to another. By setting weak or even "bad" ideas down on paper, two things are accomplished. First, these ideas may have elements which can be modified and combined to create more interesting solutions. Second, setting them down on paper can free you to begin to look for new ideas. If you hold back these seemingly weaker ideas, they can block your thinking and obstruct the ideation process. Exhausting obvious possibilities enables you to move on to different areas of speculation. This is not to say that a more obvious first idea will not be the best solution, but rather to suggest that innovative ideas are most often the result of exhaustive thought.

Only after generating as many ideas as possible

should you begin to judge them. It can be useful to set specific goals for ideation. For example, you might decide to sketch until you come up with thirty ways to answer the problem. If you judge your ideas as they are generated or proceed beyond ideation without generating a sufficient pool of ideas from which to choose, you can short-circuit your creative process.

Judgment

Having generated a range of possible responses to the problem at hand, you are now ready to *judge* them, seeking to choose the best. This choice should be based on the understanding of the problem developed during the problem definition stage. Most serious problems in the creative process arise from bad judgment. This does not necessarily mean that the decisions and choices are in and of themselves bad. Rather, the timing may be off. We may either judge too soon, during the ideation process, or not at all.

At times you may be confronted with critical choices and fail to make any judgment at all, simply accepting what you have done. This passivity may be an attempt to avoid responsibility for certain aspects of your work. The unwillingness to judge can result from a natural reluctance to find your work inadequate or to accept the need to return to an earlier stage of the design process. This is a failure of acceptance, of truly wanting to solve the problem. It is important to realize that starting over may be more expeditious than trying to repair mistakes in achieving successful results.

It is also easy to judge your work too quickly. This may be the result of impatience in trying to reach a solution or failure to take your choices seriously. Decision making is

at the very core of the design process. When you stop making choices, you cease to function as an artist or designer and reduce yourself to being a mere laborer. Design takes courage—the courage to confront what you have done and take the risk of trying things which may not work out; the courage to recognize elements of your work which are not functioning and accept the responsibility of restructuring the image until it succeeds.

Image making generally involves alternating and overlapping periods of both creativity and labor. Seldom will an artist or designer be confronted with a good idea, fully realized, requiring only simple labor for its completion. Successful work requires continuing awareness of the effectiveness of your efforts in both of these areas.

Realization

There is more to a successful work of art than merely a good idea. If all that were required were good ideas, you could ensure the quality of your work by copying the ideas of your more successful colleagues. What differentiates outstanding from mediocre work in any field is not the ideas behind it, but the *realization* of those ideas. The quality of your work will depend to a certain extent on your manual skills, how well you are able to manipulate materials, and your experience, but you should not be dismayed if you are just beginning to make images and have limited skill and experience. Skills are often best acquired "on the job," and each project you complete adds to your experience.

There are a number of ways that you can ensure that your work will be of the highest quality that you are capable of producing. Perhaps most important is to give yourself enough time. No matter how talented you are, it takes time to finish pieces which convey a sense of authority. Make preparatory drawings (Figure 4). Try out ideas and new media first in your sketchbook or outside the border of your piece. Be prepared to start over from the beginning if you make an error and are unable to make it work to your advantage.

Pause regularly. Step back from your work and ask yourself if it is accomplishing the goals you have set. Does it communicate as well from a distance as it does up close? Remember, you will have spent hours looking at your image from a distance of only a few feet. It will be judged by others looking at it from across the room for only a moment. Your work should speak for itself, without your having to explain how it was supposed to look—"What we see is what we get!" In addition, you should be attentive to

craftsmanship. The care you take in your work suggests its importance to you. Finally, you should present your finished work as professionally as possible.

Analysis

This is the final, and perhaps most important, stage of the creative process. When you have finished your work, it is time to step back and *analyze* what you have done. From this analysis can come an appreciation of the strengths and weaknesses of your current work, which will add to your experience and contribute to the foundations upon which your future work will rest. As the chart in Figure 2 indicates, analysis leads directly back into the beginning of the design process. The insights gained from critique and anal-

FIGURE 4 Keith Vaughan, *Study for Theseus, Mural, Festival of Britain*, 1951, graphite on paper, 6 × 14″. Courtesy of Austin/Desmond Fine Art.

ysis are used to redefine the problem facing the artist, delineating new challenges and enabling a new beginning. Section 3 provides specific strategies for analysis.

ART AND ATHLETICS: AN ANALOGY

The development of artistic ability may be compared to the development of athletic ability. In art as in sports, achievement is measured in terms of performance rather than training. This is not to deny the importance of training, but rather to recognize that the best coaching cannot make an outstanding athlete if the aspirant's desire and commitment

are insufficient. There are champions who overcome physical handicaps to excel and "natural athletes" who find themselves unable to compete at the college or professional level. Those who succeed are those who practice.

Artistic skill is acquired much like athletic skill. To some it seems to come naturally, but most of us are not so fortunate. Learning to make art can be likened to learning to hit a ball. You are confronted with a very complicated task requiring a developed sense of coordination and timing in a setting where failure will be instantly noted by those around you. Some freeze. Others fall back on previously learned approaches, preferring not to risk trying something new. If you decide to go ahead and try, you may be overwhelmed in the beginning by all of the things you are trying to remember. When you do hit the ball for the first time, it is with great effort and feels awkward. Hitting a ball poorly can feel like hitting a brick wall. If you are persistent in your efforts, however, you will one day begin to internalize what you have been practicing. You will hit the ball perfectly. The swing will seem effortless, and you will be unable to remember what it was you were thinking about. If you are diligent in your practice as an artist, you will internalize your lessons, and your work will, occasionally, become effortless. Unfortunately, that state of being perfectly in tune usually fades, and you must go back to your

FIGURE 5 Thomas Eakins, *Baseball Players Practicing*, 1875, watercolor, 10⅞ × 12⅞". Museum of Art, Rhode Island School of Design; Jesse Metcalf and Walter H. Kimball Funds.

exercises, working to regain the ability to perform intuitively.

You might think of school as being like spring training. An individual who is a strong fielder but a weak hitter will concentrate on batting practice. In training you work on your areas of weakness. Similarly, you should look at difficult assignments as opportunities to develop new strengths rather than as obstacles to be avoided.

Athletes exercise. They practice. In this, too, the development of artistic skills is similar to the development of athletic skills. Most of the assignments you will be given in your first year of art school are exercises. They are designed to help you develop certain abilities. A good assignment, like a good exercise, can be repeated. Athletes never stop working out, and neither should artists.

If you want to excel, you must do your best work. In the future you will be judged by the body of your work. This emphasis on your performance, as demonstrated in the objects you produce, can liberate you from focusing solely on getting good grades. Your future opportunities will be based on the impression made by your work. Just as "walk-ons" show up at tryouts without having been recruited and make the team because of their performance, so you can open doors for yourself if your portfolio is strong enough.

ABOUT COLLEGE

College is a place where people come together to learn. The word comes from the Latin *collegium*, which means colleagueship or partnership. A college may be thought of as a group of colleagues gathered together for the purpose of learning and educating themselves and one another. It is dedicated to learning rather than teaching, and this is an important distinction.

One of the benefits of coming to a school to study is the opportunity to pursue your development as an artist or designer in the company of a committed group of peers engaged in the same undertaking. Art school is distinguished from apprenticeship, with its emphasis on the one-on-one relationship between master and apprentice, by this gathering of students. Unlike the nineteenth-century academies built around the idea of training students to emulate masters, contemporary art departments depend on the free and open exchange of ideas and attitudes between students and faculty for their vitality. The quality of your college experience will depend as much on your relationships with your fellow students as it will on your relationships with your professors.

In higher education the primary responsibility for learning is placed upon the student. Professors provide their students with opportunities to learn. Their role is to challenge rather than to provide tried and true solutions. They work to create a stimulating environment where learning can flourish, and, as practicing artists, they serve as role models. It is your job to absorb as much as you can from your professors and your fellow students. Not unlike the library, they exist as resources. It is up to you to learn as much as you can from them.

2

The Glossary

The bulk of your energies in studio classes will be devoted to actually making images. You will work in response to assignments presented by your instructors, and your projects will be reviewed in regular critiques. If you are to make the most of these classes and apply the creative problem-solving strategies discussed in Section 1, it is essential that you have a broad command of the verbal and visual vocabulary of the arts. This section is designed to provide you with a basic understanding of terms that you are likely to encounter in assignments and critiques and to expose you to a sampling of modern and contemporary works of art. Terms appearing in small caps in the definitions are defined elsewhere in the glossary.

We pointed out at the end of the last section that you need to learn as much as you can from your instructors and fellow students, and while some of this learning can come from attentive observation and listening, much of it will emerge from dialogue. If you are going to communicate effectively with your colleagues, it is essential that you develop a shared vocabulary. This glossary will provide a beginning. We have intentionally limited the glossary definitions to widely used terms and have focused on definitions which reflect current usage.

Just as effective dialogue depends on a shared verbal vocabulary, so also is it enriched by a shared visual vocabulary. Often in art, we need to express ideas or concepts which words can describe only approximately. Our ability to communicate these ideas is enhanced if we are able to refer to familiar images. The illustrations in this text provide a basis for developing this shared visual vocabulary.

abstract to generalize, summarize, or distill. Abstraction takes place whenever an image is translated from one method of representation to another.

When writing a paper, you may be asked to first submit an abstract. In this context, an abstract is a brief statement which summarizes the intent of the writer and the content of the paper. An abstract of the title of a piece of property is a concise history of its ownership. Abstraction in these nonart situations requires a manner of approaching information that parallels the concerns of the artist in the studio.

Art and design can be understood in terms of degrees of visual abstraction. The form this abstraction takes varies from individual to individual and is defined by a wide variety of factors, but all art is united in that it seeks to express some essential information about the world in which it exists.

Two approaches toward abstraction can be seen in portraits by Alice Neel (Figure 6) and Willem de Kooning (Figure 7). The Neel is more NATURALISTIC than

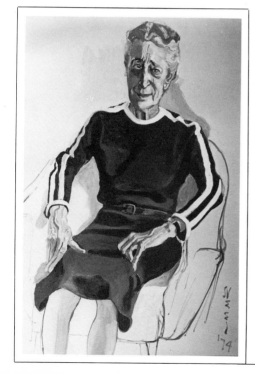

FIGURE 7 Willem De Kooning, *Woman II*, 1952, oil on canvas, 6′ 3⅞″ × 58″. Collection, The Museum of Modern Art, New York. Lillie P. Bliss Collection.

FIGURE 6 Alice Neel, *Portrait of Isabel Bishop*, 1974, oil on canvas, 44 × 30″. Collection of The Montclair Art Museum, Montclair, New Jersey.

the de Kooning, yet the modifications of visual reality are numerous. Among these modifications are an emphasis on CONTOUR, which does not occur in reality, and a concentration on detail in the hands and face relative to the other parts of the figure. There is a long tradition in portraiture of selective attention as a means of evoking the personality of the sitter. De Kooning employs a more aggressive abstraction of the figure. While in some sections he makes emphatic use of contour lines, in others he allows the figure to blur and merge with the background. Body proportions are distorted, and the placement of specific parts of the body is in response to artistically sensed appropriateness instead of objectively observed reality. This seemingly chaotic representation of the figure enables him to convey a sense of urgency and vitality that would be impossible with a more naturalistic representation.

abstract art   a term used by some to describe NONOBJECTIVE art and those modernist movements which are devoted to a high degree of abstraction. Among the movements referred to are ABSTRACT EXPRESSIONISM, CUBISM, FUTURISM, and SUPREMATISM.

Abstract Expressionism   a movement of the late 1940s and 1950s characterized by large, bold, highly ABSTRACT or NONOBJECTIVE canvases; a commitment to the importance of PROCESS; and highly subjective and introspective subject matter. The abstract expressionist movement focused international attention on New York City as a center of painting.

A major catalyst for the movement was the influx of immigrant European artists in the period immediately preceding and during World War II, bringing with them radical new ideas and concepts which challenged many of the conservative attitudes dominant in America, including REGIONALISM. Foremost among these new ideas was an emphasis on emotional involvement in the process of painting. In addition, the Abstract Expressionists were influenced by the SURREALIST emphasis on myth, the importance of the subconscious mind, and unorthodox working methods including AUTOMATISM. Abstract Expressionism placed a greater emphasis on JUNGIAN theories rather than the older FREUDIAN theories embraced by the Surrealists.

The Abstract Expressionist movement contained two related but discernibly different branches, ACTION PAINTING and COLOR FIELD PAINTING. Major artists associated with Abstract Expressionism include Willem de Kooning (Figure 7), Arshile Gorky, Adolph Gottlieb, Lee Krasner, Barnett Newman, Jackson Pollock, and Mark Rothko (Figure 8).

academic   a manner of working which recalls the training of the nineteenth-century academies such as the French Academy. Academic work is characterized by an objective approach to REPRESENTATIONAL imagery, precise draftsmanship, and carefully balanced composition. Norman Lundin's drawing (Figure 9) has strong academic qualities.

FIGURE 8 Mark Rothko, *Blue, Orange, Red*, 1961, oil on canvas, 7' 6¼" × 6' 9¼". Hirshhorn Museum and Sculpture Garden, Smithsonian Institution, Gift of the Joseph H. Hirshhorn Foundation, 1966.

FIGURE 9 Norman Lundin, *60th St. Studio: 2nd Floor, 2 Bottles*, 1983, pastel on paper, 44 × 28". Courtesy of Francine Seders Gallery; Photo by Chris Eden.

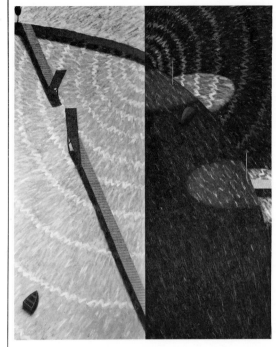

FIGURE 10 Susanne Slavick, *Open Bridge*, 1981, oil on canvas, 60 × 33″. Courtesy of Struve Gallery, Chicago.

accent   a minor contrasting element which exerts a major influence on the compositional structure of an image. In Susanne Slavick's painting (Figure 10), a number of elements function as accents to the overall structure of the image. These elements include the tree in the upper left-hand corner, the light poles along the shoreline on the right-hand side of the image, and the rowboat in the lower left-hand corner.

achromatic   literally "without CHROMA"; devoid of HUE. When the INTENSITY of a COLOR is reduced to zero, when all of its chroma is neutralized, it appears gray. An image or object may be thought of as achromatic if it is composed entirely of black, white, and gray, or of colors whose intensities are so low that hue is visually inaccessible. Black and white photography, drawings in graphite or charcoal, and prints in black or gray inks may be thought of as achromatic.

acrylic   paint which uses acrylic polymer as its BINDER. Acrylic paints may be purchased in tubes or jars, and their consistency may vary from liquid to viscous. Acrylics are quick drying compared to OIL PAINTS, and their permanence and flexibility allow them to be used in a variety of techniques and combinations. The acrylic POLYMER MEDIUM may be purchased separately and mixed with various materials to build a flexible but solid textural surface.

Action Painting   a painting style characterized by dripped, thrown, and spattered paint. "Action" Painting implies the physical action of the artist. This style emerged as an aspect of ABSTRACT EXPRESSIONISM. Because action painting employs the broad muscular gestures of the artist, works tend to be large in FORMAT. The controlled dripping and splattering of the paint places an emphasis on the process which brings the painting into being (Figure 11).

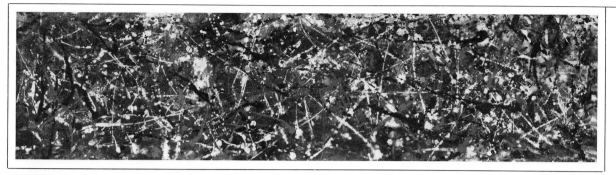

FIGURE 11 Jackson Pollock, *Number 25*,
1950, encaustic on canvas, 10⅛ × 39″.
Hirshhorn Museum and Sculpture
Garden, Smithsonian Institution, Gift of
the Joseph H. Hirshhorn Foundation,
1966.

FIGURE 12 Additive color effects.

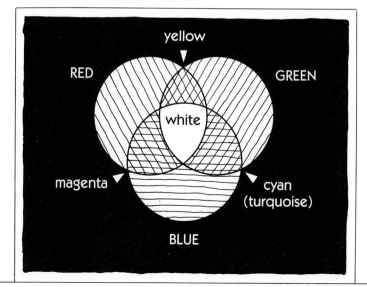

additive color　a color whose HUE is established by the
combining of MONOCHROMATIC light sources. Color
television employs additive color to create the range of
hues, values, and intensities which make up the
image. Additive color is also used in theatrical lighting, in which spotlights of the PRIMARY hues may be
overlapped to create white. The additive primary colors are *red*, *green*, and *blue*. When mixed additively,
they yield colors of higher VALUE and INTENSITY, as
illustrated in Figure 12.

aerial perspective　see *atmospheric perspective*

aesthetic　beautiful; stimulating to the senses in a manner which combines intellectual as well as perceptual
involvement.

15

aesthetics   the study of the concept of beauty, how it is defined, and how people experience and understand it.

afterimage   the phenomenon of visual perception which persists or emerges after visual stimulation is removed. Strong visual stimuli, such as bright lights or brilliant colors leave a COMPLEMENTARY afterimage. This is thought to be the result of fatiguing the sensing nerves of the eye. If you look away to a neutral ground after staring at a brilliant color, you will "see" the complement of that HUE. Similarly, staring at a bright light creates a temporary "black hole" in your field of vision.

airbrush   a tool used to apply paint or ink in a precisely controlled spray. An airbrush can be used to create uniform modulations in color. It is usually used in combination with FRISKET stencils to create hard edges.

alkyd   a painting MEDIUM in which the BINDER is an alkyd resin which combines the quick-drying qualities of ACRYLIC with the compatibility with a variety of solvents which characterizes OIL paints.

allegorical   NARRATIVE art in which the story is symbolic. An allegory may be thought of as a drawn-out metaphor. Allegorical images or stories often have a moral or ethical message. Roger Brown's painting *The Decline and Fall of the American Empire* (Figure 13) depicts the financial oppression of the common man by forces ranging from taxes in the guise of Uncle Sam to medical expenses in the figure of a doctor.

allover   an attitude toward COMPOSITION such that all parts of the image carry equal visual weight. In Mark Tobey's painting (Figure 14), the subtle differentiations of line, color, and shape working in concert with an underlying vertical/horizontal grid structure contribute to the allover compositional effect through their repetition and distribution throughout the canvas.

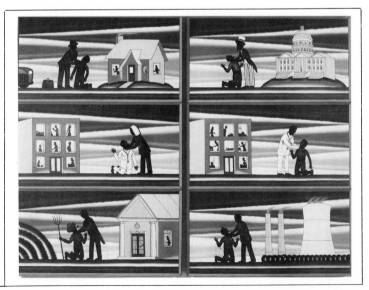

FIGURE 13 Roger Brown, *The Decline of the American Empire*, 1985, oil on canvas, two panels, 72 × 48″. Courtesy of the Phyllis Kina Gallery—Chicago/New York. Photo by William H. Bengtson.

FIGURE 14 Mark Tobey, *Multiple Still Life*, 1953, oil on canvas, 25 × 14″. Private Collection. Photo by Darrell Kirk.

amorphous   without form. Forms which are loosely, incompletely, or vaguely defined may be described as amorphous (Figure 14).

analogous colors   colors whose HUES are adjacent to one another on the circumference of the color wheel. Analogous colors are families of colors such as blues, blue-greens, and greens, or yellows, browns, and oranges (Figure 15).

analogous harmony   a color scheme which is dominated by a single group of analogous colors.

angular perspective   see *two-point perspective*

apparent color   see *perceived color*

appropriation   the taking for oneself, without permission, of the composition, imagery, style, technique, content, or other aspect of the imagery or work of others.

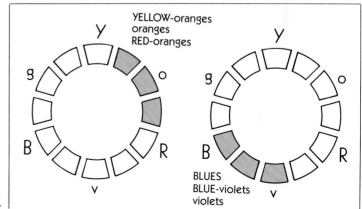

FIGURE 15 Analogous colors.

Artists employ a wide-ranging visual environment as a source for imagery and ideas. Appropriation occurs when images made by others, whether from the realm of the fine or the applied arts, are borrowed, making a purposeful reference to a shared vocabulary of visual forms.

The appropriation of any imagery from readily recognizable works draws the source and its particular meanings to the viewer's consciousness, tempering or altering the CONTENT of the new work. Edouard Manet's *Olympia* (Figure 16) outraged the public because it depicted a prostitute in a pose that traditionally suggested noble beauty. This pose mimics the poses employed by the Renaissance painters Giorgione and Titian to express concepts of love and devotion. Manet's concerns are more banal, and the painting draws power from the irony of the appropriated imagery.

Appropriation is a central aspect of the investigations of such POST-MODERNIST artists as Sherrie Levine. In her photograph *Untitled (After Walker Evans)* (Figure 17), Levine presents a direct copy of an original photograph by Walker Evans (Figure 18), one of the acknowledged masters of modern photography. Like much CONCEPTUAL ART, Levine's photograph focuses on ideas and issues beyond the object itself. She directs attention to the issue of the "masterpiece" and whether the sensations provided by the acknowledged copy are less genuine than those provided by the original. Her assault on authenticity challenges notions of value, asking whether the Evans photograph is valued because of its uniqueness or because of its ability to signify meaning through subject and form. (See also *derivation*.)

Armory Show perhaps the single most important exhibition of art in the twentieth century, this show, officially known as the International Exhibition of Modern Art and held in an armory in New York City in 1913, provided a large sector of the American press and public with an abrupt introduction to European modernist art. Although there were a number of sympathetic critics and patrons, the show generated widespread ferment, and a circuslike atmosphere

FIGURE 16 Edouard Manet, *Olympia*, 1863, oil on canvas, 51⅜ × 74¾″. Musée d'Orsay, Paris.

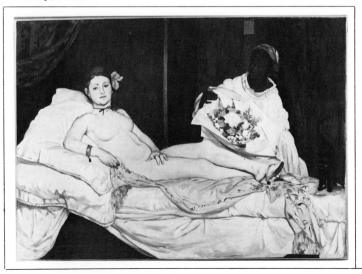

FIGURE 17 Sherrie Levine, *Untitled (After Walker Evans)*, 1981, photograph, 8 × 10″. Courtesy of Mary Boone Gallery. Photo by Zindman/Fremont.

FIGURE 18 Walker Evans, untitled photograph. Courtesy of the Library of Congress.

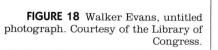

FIGURE 19 Marcel Duchamp, *Nude Descending a Staircase No. 2*, 1912, oil on canvas, 58 × 35″. Philadelphia Museum of Art: Louise and Walter Arensberg Collection.

prevailed as nearly 300,000 flocked to see works by IMPRESSIONIST, POST-IMPRESSIONIST, FAUVE, and CUBIST painters. These European (primarily French) works were regarded by many as radical; an assault on the traditions of Western art. Numerous works were subjected to specific ridicule, including Marcel Duchamp's *Nude Descending a Staircase* (Figure 19), which was called "an explosion in a shingle factory."

Art Nouveau French for "new art," a late nineteenth- and early twentieth-century movement characterized by extreme stylization, decorative organic forms, and flowing, curving lines. Art Nouveau was an international movement and is known today through the designs of Henry van de Velde (Figure 20) and the work of such artists as Aubrey Beardsley, Alphonse Mucha, Hector Guimard, and Louis Comfort Tiffany.

Ashcan School a term commonly used to refer to a group of early twentieth-century New York City painters whose subject matter focused on humble, everyday, urban sights. These painters were indebted to the tradition of mid nineteenth-century REALISM in both their choice of subject matter and in their use of lively and textural brushwork. They encountered severe criticism from some who felt that their imagery was sordid and tawdry, but the Ashcan School's affront to conservative American tastes was soon eclipsed by the presentation of modern European art in the 1913 ARMORY SHOW.

Among those artists associated with the Ashcan School are George Bellows, Robert Henri, George Luks (Figure 70), and John Sloan.

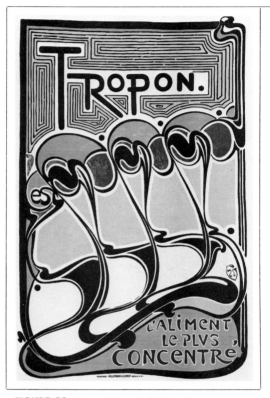

FIGURE 20 Henry Van de Velde, *Tropon, L'aliment le plus concentré* [Tropon, The Most Concentrated Nourishment], 1899, offset facsimile of original lithograph, 31⅝ × 21⅜″. Collection, The Museum of Modern Art, New York. Gift of Tropon-Werke.

asymmetrical balance balance achieved by contrasting differences in VALUE, size, or significance, independent of SYMMETRY. Degas's painting *Jockeys Before the Race* (Figure 21) is an outstanding example of asymmetrical balance. Degas establishes an off-center AXIS by placing the pole off center and proceeding to balance the vital activity of the horses with a much broader expanse of quiet and calm.

FIGURE 21 Edgar Degas, *Jockeys Before the Race*, 1869-1872, oil on paper, 42¼ × 29″. The Barber Institute of Fine Arts, The University of Birmingham.

atmospheric perspective a means of enhancing the illusion of PICTORIAL SPACE by representing the natural effect of air or atmosphere between the viewer and distant objects or forms. This is achieved by a general graying and reduction in INTENSITY and sharpness of elements within the composition as they recede into space. Objects which are close to the viewer are rendered with higher VALUE contrasts, crisper detail, and higher-intensity colors than objects at a distance. In addition, atmospheric intervention shifts HUE towards the blue or COOL side of the COLOR WHEEL.

Atmospheric perspective can be seen in Berthe Morisot's *View of Paris from the Trocadero* (Figure 22). In this freely brushed painting, the gradation of space from near to middle to far is achieved by diminishing the sharpness and detail between the foreground and middleground and representing the distant cityscape as softly defined forms bathed in an all-encompassing, purple-gray haze.

automatism a passive process of creation in which the artist allows the work to create itself, avoiding the

FIGURE 22 Berthe Morisot, *View of Paris from the Trocadero*, 1872, oil on canvas, 18¼ × 32″. Collection of the Santa Barbara Museum of Art (Gift of Mrs. Hugh N. Kirkland.)

influence of any preconceived notions of the finished piece. Chance effects, such as those employed by artists of the DADA movement, are used as a means of separating the artist's conscious control from the work at hand.

One realization of automatism is in the form of automatic drawing, where the same sensibility is applied to the making of drawings. Doodling, drawing created without conscious direction, may be thought of as a trivial form of automatic drawing. The SURREALISTS sought through automatic drawing to release potent images and forms embedded in the unconscious mind, using the process as a visual equivalent of Freud's verbal free association. (See *Freudian*.)

Avant-garde a French military term used to describe a small group of soldiers sent in advance of the larger body of troops. In art the term avant-garde describes those artists in the forefront of new activity. The avant-garde is that small group of artists which, seemingly without fear, takes artistic risks and challenges the boundaries of what is acceptable in art.

The avant-garde is associated with the very beginnings of MODERN ART. The REALIST painters Gustave Courbet and Edouard Manet were among the avant-garde of their time. Their work challenged the status quo and faced the ridicule of the art public. Their images and ideas later gained acceptance among their fellow artists and were absorbed into the larger IMPRESSIONIST movement, which continued and extended their challenges.

This same pattern has been repeated throughout the twentieth century and can be seen in the history of such avant-garde movements as CUBISM and SURREALISM. The current abundance of directions and concerns in CONTEMPORARY ART, coupled with their wide acceptance, challenges the possibility of an avant-garde today. In an age when all possibilities are open it may be impossible to find conventions to challenge or barriers to break down. (See also *Post-Modernism*.)

axis the perceived center or spine of a shape; the "dividing line" in a symmetrical image. An axis is a line around which an image or part of an image is organized.

balance the sensed structural stability resulting from looking at images in terms of gravity and physical mass and judging them against "common sense" ideas of physical structure. Balance generally refers to the relationship between the left and right sides of an image rather than between the top and bottom. It is usually the result of weighing dissimilar elements and is responsive to HUE, VALUE, INTENSITY, and SHAPE as well as *placement*.

Balance is a quality which all images have to a greater or lesser degree. The extent to which balance in a piece results from the interaction of dissimilar elements has a direct bearing on the visual excitement of the piece. Artists employ a wide range of devices and methods to achieve a desired state of balance in their works.

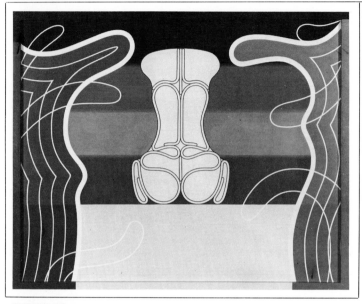

FIGURE 23 Barbara Rossi, *Icelandic*, 1981, acrylic on masonite, 28 × 35″. Courtesy of the Phyllis Kind Gallery—Chicago/New York. Photo by William H. Bengtson.

Barbara Rossi's *Icelandic* (Figure 23) achieves a strong sense of balance through the repetition of virtually identical shapes on each side of its vertical axis. (See also *asymmetrical balance*; *informal balance*; and *symmetry*.)

Bauhaus a highly influential school of art and design which was established in Germany in 1919 and continued until 1933, when it was closed by the Nazis. The school was devoted to the concept of unity and equality between artists and craftsmen and identified itself with the industrial age. It was the first school to treat the design of manufactured objects as an art. At the Bauhaus, painters and sculptors worked and studied alongside weavers and woodworkers. The Bauhaus broke with the traditional training methods used in the nineteenth-century academies. It originated the idea of a curriculum built on a shared foundation of design training for all students. Although the school encouraged stylistic independence, a Bauhaus aesthetic of reduced form, precise geometry, and limited color is discernible in many of the objects produced at the school.

Despite its relatively short existence, the Bauhaus attracted an esteemed faculty, including Josef Albers, Walter Gropius, Wasily Kandinsky, Paul Klee, Lazlo Moholy-Nagy, Ludwig Mies van der Rohe, and Oskar Schlemmer (Figure 24).

bezold effect describes the optical mixing which creates a PERCEIVED COLOR when small areas of different colors are placed adjacent to one another. The bezold effect is the primary device employed in POINTILLISM. The optical mixing yields results similar to both ADDITIVE-COLOR mixing and SUBTRACTIVE-COLOR mixing. The bezold effect creates colors with more vibrancy and INTENSITY than subtractive mixing but does not produce the higher VALUE of additive mixing. For example, when PRIMARY blue and yellow are mixed subtractively (mixing yellow and blue paint), they yield a middle-value, moderate-intensity green; mixed additively (mixing yellow and blue light), they

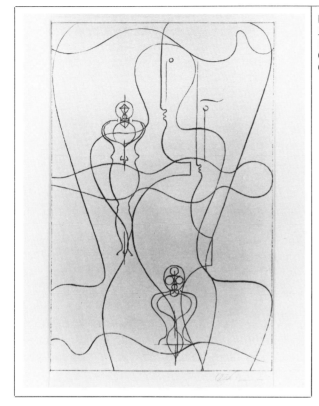

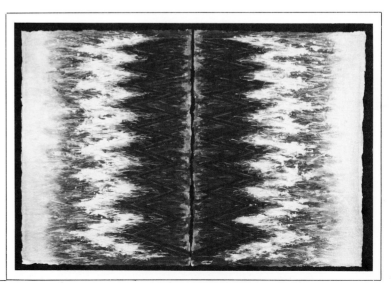

FIGURE 24 Oskar Schlemmer, *Figurenplan* [Diagram of Figures], 1919-1920, lithograph, 13⅝ × 8½". Courtesy of Worthington Gallery, Chicago, IL.

yield a high-value, moderate-intensity green; mixed by the bezold effect, they yield a moderate-value, high-intensity green.

bilateral symmetry the equal placement of visual elements on either side of a central AXIS. This creates a very stable sense of BALANCE. In Karen Guzak's *Fire Flash* (Figure 25), the two sides of the image are almost identical. One of the major sources of interest

FIGURE 25 Karen Guzak, *Fire Flash*, 1984, aqueous media on paper, 62½ × 95". Courtesy of the artist, represented by Foster/White Gallery, Seattle.

in the composition is the subtle difference between the two sides of the piece.

binder the material or MEDIUM used in paint or a drawing tool to hold the pigments in suspension allowing for their controlled distribution and adhesion to the GROUND. The effect of the binder on a medium is two-fold. The nature of the binder determines the working characteristics and feel of a particular medium. In addition, the binder surrounds the particles of pigment, controlling their exposure to the atmosphere and susceptibility to oxidation, and affects the drying properties and the transmission and reflectivity of light. Media are often defined in terms of their binders (Figure 26).

biomorphic an adjective used to describe configurations which suggest the appearance of plant or animal life, especially lower forms of life such as amoebae and other single-celled organisms.

The sharply defined, soft, curvilinear forms in the foreground of Yves Tanguy's painting (Figure 27) are biomorphic shapes that evoke a range of associations from plant forms to human anatomy. The biomorphic associations are enchanced by the contrast of these forms with their more GEOMETRIC underpinnings.

bird's-eye view a point-of-view in an image in which the scene depicted is shown from an elevated vantage point. A bird's-eye view can convey the feeling that the viewer is included in the image as an unobserved witness. Grant Wood uses a bird's-eye view to great effect in his painting (Figure 28).

FIGURE 26 Media and binders.

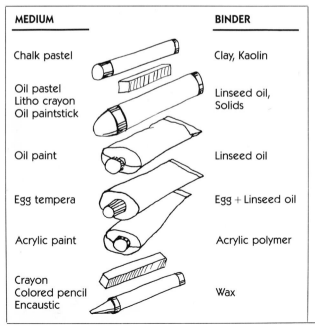

MEDIUM	BINDER
Chalk pastel	Clay, Kaolin
Oil pastel Litho crayon Oil paintstick	Linseed oil, Solids
Oil paint	Linseed oil
Egg tempera	Egg + Linseed oil
Acrylic paint	Acrylic polymer
Crayon Colored pencil Encaustic	Wax

FIGURE 27 Yves Tanguy, *Suffering Softens Stones*, oil on canvas, 36 × 28″. Krannert Art Museum, University of Illinois, Urbana-Champaign.

FIGURE 28 Grant Wood, *The Midnight Ride of Paul Revere*, 1931, oil on masonite, 30 × 40″. The Metropolitan Museum of Art, Arthur H. Hearn Fund, 1950. Estate of Grant Wood/VAGA New York 1988.

FIGURE 29 Franz Marc, *The Large Blue Horses*, 1911, oil on canvas, 41¼ × 71½". Collection, Walker Arts Center, Minneapolis. Gift of the T. B. Walker Foundation, Gilbert M. Walker Fund, 1942.

Blaue Reiter   German for "blue rider." An artists' group founded and dominated by Franz Marc (Figure 29), for whom blue was a favorite color, and Wasily Kandinsky, who employed the horse and rider as a repeated MOTIF. The Blaue Reiter was an association primarily of German EXPRESSIONIST artists founded in 1908 and active until 1910. The major focus of the group was the sponsorship of exhibitions of their own work and that of others they felt conveyed a direct, honest, and spontaneous creativity. The Blaue Reiter exhibitions were among the first to display the art of children and NAIVE painters as fine art rather than simply as curiosities.

A major difference between the Blaue Reiter and DIE BRÜCKE is the emphasis placed by the Blaue Reiter on more highly ABSTRACT and NONOBJECTIVE art. The Blaue Reiter artists also stressed a more spiritual, even mystical, basis for their art.

In addition to Marc and Kandinsky, the Blaue Reiter included Alexej Jawlensky and Gabriele Münter.

body of work   a group of works created by a single artist or a group of artists working in COLLABORATION over a specific period of time. In addition to being defined by time, a body of work may be united by issues of FORM or CONTENT as well. An artist's intent is best understood through the consideration of a body of his or her work. This is especially true of contemporary artists whose work may be self-referential and focus on very narrow areas of conceptual or visual concern. For example, Sherrie Levine's images (see APPROPRIATION) are best understood in the context of the body of her work.

border   the edge surrounding the FORMAT of an image. A border can serve to separate an image from the world around it, defining its universe, reinforcing its shape, and providing context for its color, texture, and imagery.

The border of an image may become a decorative field in and of itself and be embellished by the artist as an integral part of the finished work, as in Figures 30 and 31.

FIGURE 31 Bert Long, *Search*, 1987, mixed media, 44½ × 26″. Courtesy of L.A. Louver Gallery, Venice, California. Photo by William Nettles.

FIGURE 30 Jim Nutt, *Another Mistake*, 1983, acrylic on masonite and wood, 24⅞ × 26¾″. Courtesy of the Phyllis Kind Gallery—Chicago/New York. Photo by William H. Bengtson.

FIGURE 32 Andrew Stevovich, *Gamblers*, 1986, oil on linen, 12 × 15″. Private collection, Canada. Courtesy of Coe Kerr Gallery Inc.

Additionally, a border acting as the edge of the format generally functions either as a "window" into the PICTORIAL SPACE of the image, or a frame surrounding the image. When the image depicted employs tight CROPPING, as in Andrew Stevovich's *Gamblers* (Figure 32), we relate to the border as a window. When the image within the picture stands apart from the border, as in the Alice Neel portrait (Figure 6), we relate to it as a frame.

bristol board a widely used drawing SUPPORT made by pressing several layers or plies of paper together. Bristol board is composed entirely of one material of uniform quality. It is much favored for fine rendering and pen-and-ink drawing. It is generally available in COLD PRESS, a slightly textured surface also referred to as *vellum*, and HOT PRESS, a smooth surface also referred to as *plate*.

Brücke, die German for "the bridge." Die Brücke was an artistic community organized in Dresden, Germany, in 1905. The four founders were young architecture students who turned to painting, sculpture, and WOODCUT as more potent vehicles for their personal expressions. They announced their intentions to forge a new link to the creative future through a revolutionary art of intense feeling. The agitated and intensely colored surfaces of Die Brücke canvases challenged the established ACADEMIC traditions which dominated German art of the time. Die Brücke artists' bold distortions of form and liberation of color beyond its descriptive function for expressive means were first influenced by Edward Munch and the POST-IMPRESSIONIST canvases of Paul Gauguin, and Vincent van Gogh. Later the FAUVE movement, CUBISM, and FUTURISM made an impact on their paintings. PRIMITIVE ART, particularly African sculpture, also held great significance for Die Brücke artists.

Among the founders of Die Brücke were Erich Heckel and Ernst Ludwig Kirchner (Figure 33). Artists later associated with the group included Otto Mueller, Emil Nolde, and Max Pechstein. (See also *Expressionism, German*.)

FIGURE 33 Ernst Ludwig Kirchner, *Street, Dresden*, 1908, dated on painting 1907, oil on canvas, 59¼″ × 6′ 6⅞″. Collection, The Museum of Modern Art, New York. Purchase.

calligraphy elegant handwriting. An expressive line having the qualities of handwriting—flow, grace, rhythm, repetition of shapes, and variation in weight. Additionally, a line or lines having the qualities of calligraphy (Figure 34). Ray George contrasts GEOMETRIC lines with softer, calligraphic lines (Figure 35).

FIGURE 34 Mark Tobey, *Pacific Transition*, 1943, gouache on paper, 23¼ × 31¼″. The Saint Louis Art Museum (Gift of Joseph Pulitzer, Jr.)

FIGURE 35 Ray George, *Utica #2*, 1983, charcoal, graphite, and acrylic on paper, 45 × 56″. Courtesy of the artist.

canvas   a relatively heavy fabric made of tightly woven cotton or flax used as a SUPPORT for painting. When flax is used, the canvas is referred to as *linen*. Canvas may also refer to any fabric used as a support for painting or to a painting on a fabric support.

cartoon   a preliminary SKETCH at full size prepared by an artist to aid in visualization and guide in the creation of a complex work such as a FRESCO or tapestry.

casein   a paint in which the BINDER is a protein derived from milk mixed with water and ammonium carbonate. True casein is rarely found anymore due to its short shelf life, and it has largely been replaced by ACRYLIC polymer paints.

chalk   a drawing material made from soft limestone pressed into sticks. The limestone may be dyed or mixed with pigments to create colored chalks.

charcoal   a black, porous, carbon drawing material made from finely charred wood. Charcoal is available in a variety of forms. Vine charcoal is made by charring fine sticks, usually willow, in a kiln. Compressed charcoal is made by combining charcoal powder and a BINDER and pressing them into sticks. It is available in a variety of hardnesses. Compressed charcoal is also available in pencils.

chiaroscuro   Italian for "light–dark." Chiaroscuro describes the use of contrasting areas of high and low values to create dramatic effects. Randy Hayes's large pastel drawing (Figure 36) relies heavily on the use of chiaroscuro to activate the individual figures as well as the composition as a whole.

chroma   see *intensity*

classical   having the qualities generally associated with the art of ancient Greece and Rome at the height of their civilizations. The artists of antiquity sought to make ideal images by abstracting the essential qualities of man and nature. Their work conveys a feeling of nobility and elegance and is characterized by a

FIGURE 36 Randy Hayes, *Pretender*, 1983, pastel on paper, 82 × 118″. Courtesy Linda Farris Gallery, Seattle.

FIGURE 37 Pablo Picasso, *A Woman in White*, 1923, oil on canvas 39 × 31½". The Metropolitan Museum of Art, Rogers Fund, 1951, Acquired from the Museum of Modern Art, Lillie P. Bliss Collection (53.140.4). All rights reserved, The Metropolitan Museum of Art.

refined sense of balance and proportion. Picasso's classical portrait of a young women (Figure 37) combines a fresh, candid vision with an abstraction and generalization of forms, creating an idealized and harmonious whole.

cold press a method of making paper or board by subjecting it to pressure without heat, yielding a moderately textured surface. Cold-pressed papers are more absorbent and have more tooth, or texture, than HOT-PRESSED papers.

collaboration the process or product of a group of individuals working together toward a single goal.

Designers and artists are usually thought of as working alone. Creativity is associated with uniqueness and individuality. In fact, designers often work in teams and almost always collaborate with a client. Working collaboratively can stimulate a cross-fertilization of ideas, capitalizing on the uniqueness of each individual's vision and skills.

Until the twentieth century, fine art, even when made through collective efforts, was almost always attributed to a single individual. During and immediately following World War I, some of the artists of DADA and SURREALISM began to make works together as well as to share ideas. Their collaboration was in part an effort to move the focus of art away from the personality of the individual artist and toward the object and its evocative qualities.

This tradition of collaboration has extended into contemporary times, and there are a number of artists who work together as collaborative teams. Among these are Gilbert and George, Komar and Melamid, and McDermott and McGough (Figure 38).

In addition to these partnerships, artists may collaborate with others, including those working in other media, on an occasional basis. For example, painters may collaborate with poets on books or work with producers in the design of theatrical productions (Figure 39).

collage from the French *coller*, meaning to paste, glue, or adhere. A collage is an image made in whole or in part by adhering a variety of two-dimensional materials to a SUPPORT. The practice was adopted in the fine arts by the CUBISTS.

The materials used in a collage may be printed materials drawn from the external world which maintain their legibility, such as receipts or fragments of magazine pages; they may be unique images, such as pieces of drawings or paintings; or they may simply be pieces of colored or textured material chosen for their decorative potential. The introduction of real materials into a context we generally associate with illusionistic representation suggests multiple levels of reality. A collage brings together materials from widely varying contexts to create a new pictorial reality. Collage makes its impact through the juxtaposition of images from varying contexts and our recognition of their original sources.

The greatest challenge in creating effective collages is to unify material from divergent contexts (Figure 40).

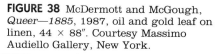

FIGURE 38 McDermott and McGough, *Queer—1885*, 1987, oil and gold leaf on linen, 44 × 88″. Courtesy Massimo Audiello Gallery, New York.

FIGURE 39 Set design for *Tristan und Isolde* by David Hockney, Los Angeles Music Center Opera, 1987. Courtesy The Los Angeles Music Center Opera. Photo by Frederic Ohringer.

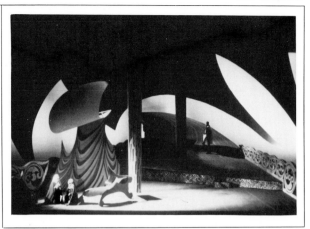

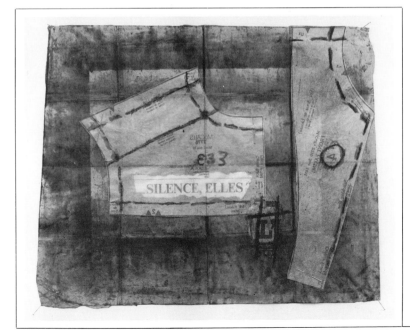

FIGURE 40 Louise Paillé, *"Lettre à" #3*, 1985, mixed media on paper, 69 × 76 cm. Courtesy of Galerie Aubes 3935, Montreal. Photo by Yvan Boulerice.

collagraphy a RELIEF printmaking method in which a COLLAGE is used as the printing plate. The collage is generally built up out of relatively thick materials such as cardboard, sandpaper, wallpaper, or fabric. The collage may be sealed with several coats of POLYMER MEDIUM to protect it from damage by ink and solvents.

color the response of the eye to electromagnetic radiation in the visual range (wavelengths from approximately 4,000 angstroms for violet light to 7,200 angstroms for red light). Just as there is sound outside our audible range, so is there light outside our visual range. Just below the violet range is ultraviolet, then X-rays, and finally gamma rays; beyond the visible red are infrared, microwaves, and finally radio waves. A color has three dimensions: HUE, VALUE, and INTENSITY. Color names describe a specific blend of these dimensions (Figure 41).

Color Field painting a painting style which emerged from ABSTRACT EXPRESSIONISM. It is characterized by large canvases with broad expanses of color in continuous, uniform surfaces or "fields" with subtle modulation. The fields of color may be punctuated by occasional stripes of contrasting color crossing the canvas; they may flow and expand into broadly defined areas or may be limited only by the edge of the canvas. In Color Field painting, the large scale of the canvas and the expansive color surfaces engulf the viewer with a sensation of homogeneous color and can inspire a sense of awe and spiritual transcendence. Major Color Field painters include Helen Frankenthaler, Barnett Newman, and Mark Rothko (Figure 8).

color temperature a scientific description of the color of radiant light. All matter radiates light when heated to a high enough temperature. This is what we see when steel is "red-hot." In art and design color tem-

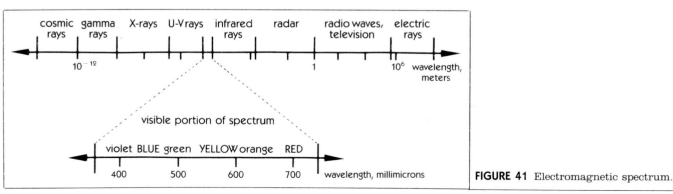

FIGURE 41 Electromagnetic spectrum.

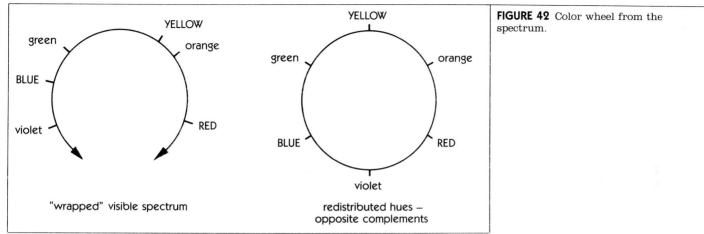

FIGURE 42 Color wheel from the spectrum.

perature is used more generally to refer to WARM and COOL colors.

color wheel a chart showing the interrelationships of colors. It is formed by wrapping the visual spectrum into a circle and distributing the hues so that COMPLEMENTS will be opposite one another on the wheel (Figure 42). The color wheel is a useful tool for exploring the relationships between colors and the results of mixing colors.

In addition to charting the hues by their placement around the circumference of the color wheel, intensities are located along the radii or spokes of the wheel, with the lowest intensity of each hue placed at the center of the wheel.

The color wheel functions as a graph of two dimensions of COLOR: HUE and INTENSITY. The result of mixing two colors of paint can be anticipated by drawing a line between the two colors on the color wheel.

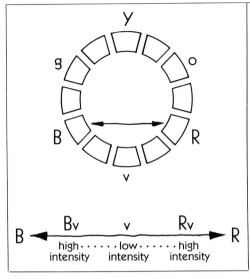

FIGURE 43 Color wheel as mixing chart.

The points along the line will match the range of hues and intensities that would result from mixing the two colors in varying proportions (Figure 43).

There have been many variations on the color wheel since Issac Newton first suggested that the visual spectrum could be effectively presented in a circle, but the one currently referred to most often is a twelve-hue wheel (Figure 44).

complement literally "to complete." The complement of red is green (yellow-blue). Any color with its complement provides all of the primary hues; thus, they are complements—they complete one another (Figure 45). (*Note*: compl**e**ment is not the same as compl**i**lment.) The complement of a HUE is that hue which lies directly across from it on the COLOR WHEEL. When a

FIGURE 44 Color wheel variations.

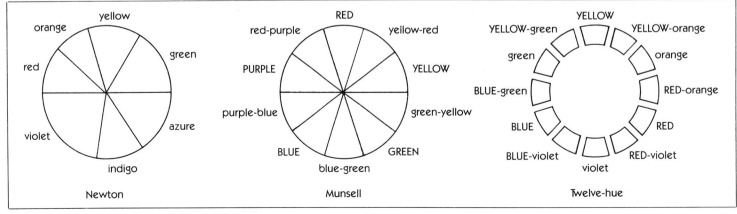

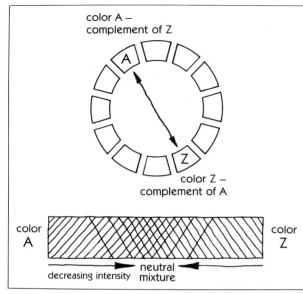

FIGURE 45 Complementary harmony.

hue is mixed with its complement in equal strength, the result is a NEUTRAL COLOR. When a small amount of its complement is added to a color, its INTENSITY will be reduced without any shift in its hue. A color wheel is arranged so that a complementary relationship exists between any two hues which lie directly opposite one another on the color wheel.

complementary harmony a color HARMONY built around the relationship of a pair of complementary hues.

composition the formal arrangement of the visual elements within an image. Composition is distinct from CONTENT.

compositional device a visual technique used to accomplish a FORMAL goal or the contrived placement of an object to create a formal effect or to affect the visual flow of an image. In James Valerio's *Cat's Cradle* (Figure 46), the BIRD'S-EYE VIEW and the arrange-

FIGURE 46 James Valerio *Cat's Cradle*, 1980, oil on canvas, 72 × 82″. Courtesy of Struve Gallery, Chicago. Photo by Quiriconi-Tropea Photographers.

ment of the glasses, scissors, and string in the foreground may be looked at as compositional devices. The point of view allows us to look into, rather than through, the scene. The small still life in the foreground echoes the poses and physical interaction of the couple.

Conceptual Art   a contemporary art movement based on the principle that the true substance of art is ideas and concepts rather than images or artifacts. Joseph Kosuth presents three representations of the concept "chair" in his piece which brings together a photograph, a physical object, and a dictionary definition (Figure 47). Many conceptual artists are opposed to creating permanent artifacts. They often provide DOCUMENTATION as the only lasting physical product of their work. Throughout the twentieth century, there has been a continuing insistence by some that art is not primarily a product of craftsmanship or technique, but rather of the creative powers of the intellect. The first movement to focus specifically on ideas rather than artisanship was DADA.

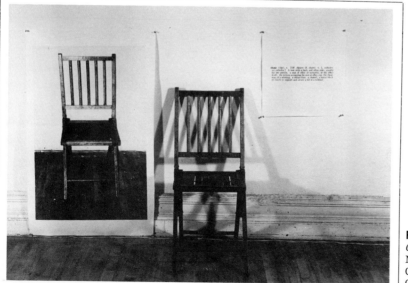

FIGURE 47 Joseph Kosuth, *One and Three Chairs*, 1965, Collection of the Museum of Modern Art, Photo courtesy of Leo Castelli Gallery, New York. Photo by Jay Cantor.

Constructivism a Russian art movement of the late 1910s and early 1920s concerned with the union of art, engineering, and technology. The founder of Constructivism, Vladimir Tatlin, was influenced by CUBISM and FUTURISM, and particularly by Cubist COLLAGE. He began to explore the use of new and unorthodox building materials, at first combined in NONOBJECTIVE sculptural reliefs, and later in architectural projects. The movement encountered government resistance in the early 1920s but continued to exert an influence outside of the Soviet Union. Many artists of the BAUHAUS subscribed to the Constructivist belief in the social responsibility of the artist.

Conté crayon a drawing medium in stick form, which uses a gum BINDER. Conté crayons are made in France by Conté à Paris and are available in white, sepia, sanguine, and black. They are widely used as an alternative to charcoal for broad gestural drawing and sketching.

contemporary art the art of our own times; used to describe art created since 1945.

content the subject matter, meaning, and cultural context of a work of art. A thorough study of the content of an object extends beyond its appearance to a consideration of the artist's entire BODY OF WORK and his or her place in time and culture.

contour the edge of a SHAPE or FORM.

contour line a line which describes or follows the edge of a shape or form—an outline. Alternately, a line which follows and reveals form, as the lines in a contour map.

cool color a color whose hue is in the lower end of the spectrum: blue-violet, blue, or blue-green (Figure 48). Cool colors tend to be perceived as receding spatially.

critique an analysis of strengths and weaknesses, with emphasis on recognizing strategies for overcoming weaknesses and achieving goals (see Section 3).

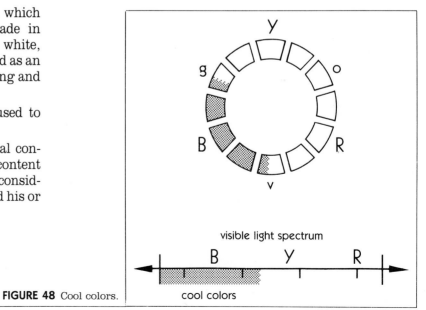

FIGURE 48 Cool colors.

FIGURE 49 Andrew Keating, *Barren Orchards*, 1985, acrylic on canvas, 36 × 60″. Courtesy of Linda Farris Gallery, Seattle.

cropping   the abrupt termination of forms or objects by the edge of the FORMAT or another object. Cropping reinforces the idea of format as a windowlike construction through which the image is seen and the concept of the image as part of a wider world which continues beyond the confines of the picture. Additionally, cropping can create interesting NEGATIVE SHAPES, thus helping to activate the background areas of a picture.

Cropping is effective because of our innate desire to see things as simply and completely as possible. Andrew Keating makes extensive use of cropping in his painting *Barren Orchards* (Figure 49). The heads and arm are cropped by the edge of the format; the hand and the scene outside the window are cropped by the drapery. Rather than leaving us wondering what the rest of the scene or the figures look like, this cropping engages our imagination to complete the image.

Similarly, the figure in Gwen Knight's drawing (Figure 50) is understood as complete. The cropping of her knee and foot do not suggest a kneeless figure, but rather tie the image into the format, activating the entire surface. Another effect of tight cropping is to bring the viewer and image together. Tight cropping can convey the feeling that the viewer and the image occupy the same space.

cropping frame a pair of L-shaped planes which are moved about over a preliminary image to explore possible compositions or formats. An empty frame (sometimes called a *viewfinder*) such as a slide mount can also be used as a cropping frame to explore variations in composition within a fixed format (Figure 51).

FIGURE 50 Gwen Knight, *Figure Study #6*, 1975, charcoal on paper, 25 × 19″. Courtesy of Francine Seders Gallery, Seattle. Photo by Chris Eden.

FIGURE 51 Cropping frame.

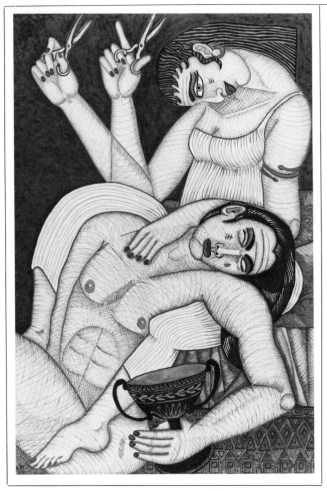

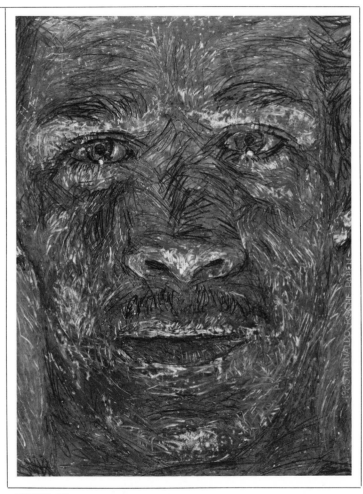

FIGURE 52 Michael Ehle, *Samson and Delilah*, 1987, gouache on paper, 30 × 44″. Courtesy of Greg Kucera Gallery, Seattle.

FIGURE 53 Arnoldo Roche Rabell, *Self Portrait*, 1985, oil on paper, 24½ × 18½″. Courtesy of Struve Gallery, Chicago.

croquis a quick SKETCH or GESTURE DRAWING, often at small scale.

cross-hatching a MODELING technique characterized by the use of straight parallel lines which cross over one another. Variations in the density of the hatching lines create differences in VALUE, while their direction can be used to enhance the illusion of volume. Michael Ehle (Figure 52) and Arnoldo Roche Rabell (Figure 53) rely on cross-hatching as their primary means of modeling.

Cubism an early twentieth-century art movement initiated by Georges Braque and Pablo Picasso. Cubism offered a complete break with the Renaissance conception of PICTORIAL SPACE as a unified whole, subject to consistent mathematical laws of perspective. The Renaissance notion of the PICTURE PLANE as a "window into the world," in which objects recede into space and diminish in size according to the rules of ATMOSPHERIC and LINEAR PERSPECTIVE, is challenged by the shallow space of Cubism. Cubist images present simultaneous images of objects from multiple points of view, fragmented and faceted forms, and a confusion of POSITIVE and NEGATIVE SHAPE relationships (Figure 54). Cubism offers an intellectual ordering, rather than a purely optical rendering, of the interrelationships of forms in a composition. Cubist COLLAGE was an invention responsive to this new approach to form and the structure of composition.

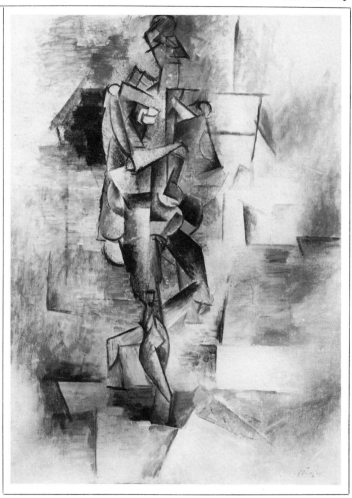

FIGURE 54 Pablo Picasso, *Female Nude*, 1909-1910, oil on canvas, 28¾ × 21¼". The Menil Collection, Houston.

Cubist painters were influenced by the shifting perspectives of Paul Cezanne's paintings and the DISTORTION of the human figure in African and primitive sculpture.

In addition to Picasso and Braque, artists associated with the movement include Marcel Duchamp (Figure 19), Albert Gleizes, Juan Gris, and Fernand Leger (Figure 96). Cubism held tremendous implications for the development of ABSTRACT painting and sculpture.

Dada an international art movement which placed its emphasis on the idea of art rather than art objects. Dada was launched in Switzerland by writers and visual artists as a protest against the First World War and the materialistic culture they felt caused it. The name for the group, French for "hobby-horse," was reportedly chosen at random from a dictionary, reflecting the playfulness and spontaneity which characterized the group's challenge to the seriousness of making art. The members of the group called themselves "Dadas." They sought to make it clear that their movement was not another "-ism," but a total way of living. In their revolt, the Dadas opened a new awareness of creative investigation and forced a reevaluation of the definitions and boundaries of art.

Jean Arp was one of the first Dadas. His experiments involving AUTOMATISM, and specifically those involving COLLAGES made by dropping papers to form random arrangements (Figure 55), are indicative of Dada's challenge to the notion of the artist as a gifted individual, uniquely able to craft an object of artistic merit. His concerns placed new emphasis on

FIGURE 55 Jean Arp, *Arrangement According to the Laws of Chance*, 1916-1917, torn and pasted papers on paper, 19⅛ × 13⅝". Collection, The Museum of Modern Art, New York. Purchase.

the PROCESS of making art as opposed to the finished object.

In his paintings and "readymades," objects taken from a nonart context and exhibited as art objects, Marcel Duchamp, the most significant figure to emerge from the Dada movement, challenged the hierarchy separating "art" experiences from "life" experiences. He forced a new intellectual involvement on the part of the viewer, a questioning of aesthetic values, tastes, and propriety.

Dada poses questions of extreme pertinence to contemporary artists. The POP ART emphasis on the merger of art and life, and the concerns for idea rather than object which distinguish CONCEPTUAL ART are indicative of Dada's influence.

Other artists associated with Dada include Max Ernst, Francis Picabia, and Man Ray.

decoration surface embellishment, often in the form of PATTERN and having little or no significant CONTENT.

decorative having as its primary purpose to decorate, embellish, or adorn. *Decorative* may be used in a pejorative sense to describe images which rely exclusively on appealing to the eye of the viewer, with little or no attempt to convey substantive meaning or message. Works such as this are often superficial, formulaic, and contrived.

Many artists, however, place great emphasis on developing the decorative qualities of their work. Steven Heyman's painting (Figure 56) has a highly embellished surface which is central to the effect of the

painting. The ALLOVER pattern unites foreground and background, confusing the space and giving the painting a two-dimensional, flat quality which works in contrast to the artist's use of OVERLAPPING and LINEAR PERSPECTIVE to suggest spatial relationships within the piece.

FIGURE 56 Steven Heyman, *Untitled*, 1981, acrylic on canvas, 59 × 59″. Courtesy of Zolla/Lieberman Gallery.

derivative a term used to describe works which are derived from external sources. Derivative work results from a thoughtful analysis of images created by others and the use of that analysis as a springboard for the creation of original works. Elaine de Kooning's DIP-TYCH (Figure 57) is derived from the prehistoric cave paintings at Lascaux. Derivation is distinguished from APPROPRIATION by the attitude and intent of the artist.

designer's colors opaque, water-based paints, usually GOUACHE.

diptych a painting created on two separate panels and meant to be viewed as a single unit. A diptych may be composed as a single harmonious whole, or the artist may use the diptych form to reinforce the juxtaposition of two images contrasting in form or content. Elaine de Kooning (Figure 57) takes the first approach, while David Salle's work (Figure 58) is an extreme example of the second.

FIGURE 57 Elaine De Kooning, *Calcium Wall (Cave #66)*, 1986, acrylic on canvas, two panels, both 84 × 66″. Courtesy of Wright Gallery, Dallas.

FIGURE 58 David Salle, *Footmen*, 1986, oil, wood bowl on canvas, 93 × 120″, two panels. Courtesy of Mary Boone Gallery, Photo by Zindman/Fremont.

FIGURE 59 Andrew Keating, *Still Life II*, 1982-1983, acrylic on canvas, 45 × 45″. Courtesy Linda Farris Gallery, Seattle.

distortion the alteration of shape in a manner which changes internal relationships and relative PROPORTIONS between parts. Intentional distortion can introduce a SURREAL quality to an image, as in Figure 59.

documentation images which record an artist's process and concepts. Documentation is often the only marketable product produced by CONCEPTUAL artists. The environmental artist Christo, a gifted and prolific draftsman, records his works in the form of drawings, prints, and films (Figures 60 and 61).

drawing the act, technique, or product of creating an image using pigment in a solid as opposed to fluid BINDER. Common MEDIA for drawing include CHALK, CHARCOAL, GRAPHITE, and SILVERPOINT.

Drawings are often defined by the interaction of linear elements. For this reason, images created with fluid media, such as ink, may be referred to as drawings if they have strong linear qualities.

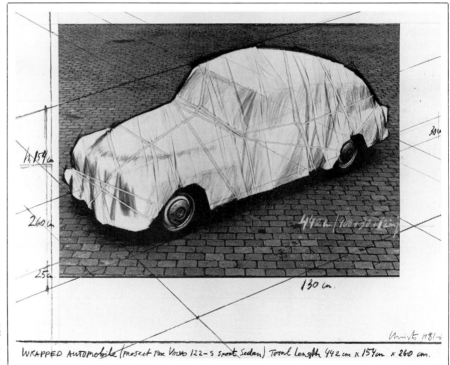

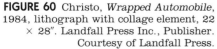

FIGURE 60 Christo, *Wrapped Automobile*, 1984, lithograph with collage element, 22 × 28". Landfall Press Inc., Publisher. Courtesy of Landfall Press.

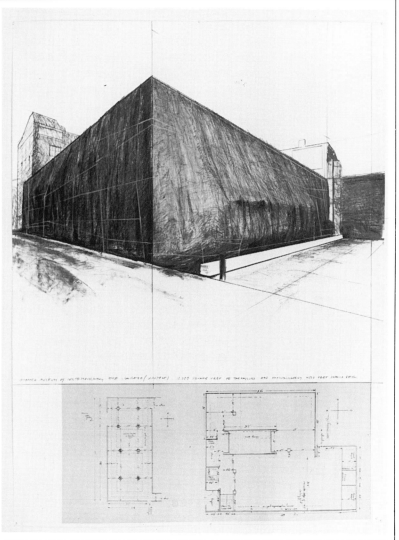

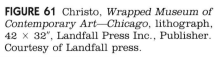

FIGURE 61 Christo, *Wrapped Museum of Contemporary Art—Chicago*, lithograph, 42 × 32″, Landfall Press Inc., Publisher. Courtesy of Landfall press.

drypoint an INTAGLIO technique in which the surface of the plate, usually a soft metal such as copper or zinc, is scratched directly with a sharp metal point. During the printing process, the ink is held in the rough burr raised by the steel needle, yielding a delicate linear image. The fragility of the burr limits drypoint to a relatively small number of impressions without loss of detail and clarity.

earth color brown. Earth colors are low INTENSITY, WARM colors. They were originally made from mineral pigments such as iron oxide or clays. Sienna was made from clay mined in Sienna, Italy, while the clay used for umber was mined in Umbria. When the pure clay is ground and no further treatment is used, the resulting pigment is called "raw." If the clay is first heated to a temperature of several hundred degrees, the resulting lower-value pigment is called "burnt."

Common earth colors are raw sienna, raw umber, burnt sienna, burnt umber, and yellow ochre.

easel painting painting at a scale such that the perimeter of the SUPPORT is within the physical reach of the artist. The support is generally a stretched canvas or a rigid panel which may easily be moved by the artist. It is usually placed on an easel for painting.

Created at a personal and intimate scale, easel painting is distinguished from large-scale works which are conceived from the outset for display in museums or other public spaces.

egg tempera see *tempera*

encaustic a painting, medium, or technique in which the BINDER is wax. In order to work with encaustic, the medium is softened and colors are mixed on a hotplate or griddle. Contemporary artists working in encaustic often combine resins with the wax to increase the hardness and permanence of the finished piece. Encaustic allows the development of a distinctive luminosity and can suggest an almost tactile depth.

engraving an INTAGLIO printmaking technique in which the image to be printed is cut or scratched into the printing plate with a sharp tool.

etching an INTAGLIO printmaking technique in which acid is used to cut the image to be printed into the printing plate. The image is controlled by the use of a RESIST which protects areas of the plate from the acid. The term also refers to a print made by this technique.

Expressionism, German a movement originating at the beginning of the century, which stressed that art must be responsive to inner necessities, to the subjective and obsessive psychological demands of the individual. In contrast to such artists as the FAUVES, who worked from a more psychologically tempered point of view, the German Expressionists employed strident color and distorted forms as metaphors for their inner turmoil. While NONOBJECTIVE painting was an outgrowth of the later years of the movement, the artists of the early years worked with REPRESENTATIONAL imagery, most often based on human situations and interactions.

Artists associated with the movement include those of DIE BRÜCKE and the BLAUE REITER.

expressionistic a term used to describe work which

conveys a sense of the emotional involvement of the artist and his or her personal responses to subject matter or media. Expressionistic work is characterized by the intensity of its presentation. Robert Arneson's *Club Social* (Figure 62) has strong expressionistic qualities in its bold forms and agitated line.

Fauvism   an early twentieth-century French art movement characterized by the expressive effects of strident color frequently applied in bold, free IMPASTO brushwork. The name "Fauve," which literally means "wild beast," was applied to the artists of the movement in criticism of their violent distortions of form and crude juxtapositions of intense color.

FIGURE 62 Robert Arneson, *Club Social*, 1983, mixed media on paper, 30 × 22". Courtesy of Struve Gallery, Chicago.

FIGURE 63 Henri Matisse, *Blue Nude (Souvenir de Biskra"), 1907, oil on canvas, 36¼ × 55¼". The Baltimore Museum of Art: The Cone Collection, formed by Dr. Claribel Cone and Miss Etta Cone of Baltimore, Maryland. (BMA 1950.228)*

Henri Matisse (Figure 63) was the most important Fauve painter. Others associated with this relatively small group were André Derain, Maurice Vlaminck, and Georges Rouault.

figurative   depicting or suggesting animate beings. The term is used frequently to refer to imagery based on the human body. Kenneth Callaghan's painting (Figure 64) has strong figurative qualities.

figure/ground   the relationship between what is perceived as object or subject and background or context. Michael Spafford focuses on figure/ground relationships in his print from the series *Thirteen Ways of Looking at a Blackbird* (Figure 65). In the upper part of the image, we see the dark chevron as figure against a light ground whereas in the lower part, the light curve emerges as figure against a dark ground.

FIGURE 64 Kenneth Callagahan, *Apocalypse*, 1949, tempera, 11½ × 37″. Private Collection. Photo by Darrell Kirk.

FIGURE 65 Michael Spafford, "Twelve," from the series *Thirteen Ways of Looking at a Blackbird*, 1986, woodblock print, 15 × 15″. Courtesy of Francine Seders Gallery, Seattle. Photo by Chris Eden.

What we see as figure and what we see as ground are determined by a complex set of perceptual principles studied in depth by the GESTALT psychologists. Foremost among these principles is the desire of the mind to understand visual phenomena as simply as possible. In order to do this, we rely on a number of visual clues to direct our attention to that which is figure or foreground in our perceptual environment and filter out that which is background. Jean Dubuffet presents a constantly shifting field of figure/ground relationships in his piece (Figure 103).

film color the perceived effect created when an object is illuminated by light of a single HUE, causing the object to appear as if it were being viewed through a colored film. Film color describes the effect of light on a white house at sunset. The LOCAL COLOR of the house is altered by the sunset, which gives it a pink PERCEIVED COLOR.

flat shallow PICTORIAL SPACE. Flat images have a "pulled to the surface" quality which is often accomplished by the use of unmodulated color and the absence of MODELING. In Jacob Lawrence's *Tools* (Figure 66), the sense of flatness is enhanced by the filling of the format with forms from top to bottom of the composition. The similarity in size of the shapes in the upper half of the image coupled with the absence of strong ORTHOGONALS limits our sense of LINEAR PERSPECTIVE in the work, contributing to the feeling of flatness.

FIGURE 66 Jacob Lawrence, *Tools*, 1978, lithograph, 26 × 21¾″. Courtesy of Francine Seders Gallery, Seattle. Photo by Chris Eden.

FIGURE 67 Michael Nakoneczny, *Flesh Fire*, 1985, acrylic on masonite, 23½ × 30½". Courtesy of Zolla/Lieberman Gallery.

focal point   the perceived focus of interest; the visual center of an image. The focal point of an image may be a specific element, such as the central figure in Michael Nakoneczny's painting (Figure 67); it may lie in a general area, as in Roger Shimomura's painting (Figure 68), where the focal point is just to the right of center; or it may be diffuse, as in Matt Straub's painting (Figure 69).

folk art   art produced by artists having no formal academic training. Folk art is highly stylized and is associated with specific social circumstances. It relates to a tradition that has evolved over time, passed from generation to generation. It often has a direct and unschooled appearance which makes it, like PRIMITIVE ART, an attractive source for artists. Folk art is distinct from NAIVE ART in that while naive art is

FIGURE 68 Roger Shimomura, *Untitled*, 1984, acrylic on canvas, 60 × 72″. Courtesy of Greg Kucera Gallery, Seattle.

FIGURE 69 Matt Straub, *The Sea Received Aim*, 1987, oil on canvas, 51 × 71″. Courtesy of Marianne Deson Gallery.

often similar in appearance, it is associated with personal and individual vision. The folk artist's work is integral to his or her society, while the naive artist acts as an individual.

foreshortening　the compression and adjustment of proportion required to NATURALISTICALLY represent in two dimensions objects which are receding in space.

Figure 70 employs forshortening in the torso of the pinned wrestler.

form　the general structure and organization of an image or part of an image. Form refers primarily to SHAPE but also to COLOR, TEXTURE, and *manner of representation*.

FIGURE 70 George Luks, *The Wrestlers*, 1905, oil on canvas, 48¼ × 66¼″. Courtesy, Museum of Fine Arts, Boston. Charles Henry Hayden Fund.

formal pertaining to the visually perceived qualities of a work of art, independent of issues of CONTENT or meaning. When we discuss the formal characteristics of a work of art, we are concerned with the FORMAL ELEMENTS and their interaction.

formal elements the elements which contribute to the visual structure of an image: COLOR, LINE, SHAPE, SPACE, TEXTURE, and VALUE. Taken together, the formal elements make up the composition of an image.

format the dimensions or proportions of a two-dimensional image. In photography format refers to the size of the film (e.g., 35mm, 2 x 2, 8 x 10, etc.). In other two-dimensional work it refers to the size of the finished piece and its orientation (i.e., horizontal or vertical).

  Format is a primary design decision, and all compositional choices are affected by it (see also *scale*; *proportion*).

framing see *cropping frame*

fresco a MURAL painting technique in which PIGMENT suspended in limewater is painted directly onto plaster built up on a wall. Because the pigment penetrates into the wet plaster rather than simply adhering to the surface, fresco is exceptionally stable.

Freudian pertaining to the psychoanalytic theories of Sigmund Freud. Freud's theories traced neurotic behavior to psychic traumas, real or imagined, early in life. He developed the technique of free association to bring repressed information out of the unconscious mind. Freudian theory presents an image of man as a bundle of instincts, driven by sexual energy. Freud introduced models of the mind divided into the conscious and the unconscious, and the personality divided into the ego, superego, and id.

  In *The Interpretation of Dreams*, published in 1900, Freud emphasized the symbolic meaning of dreams as a key to the unconscious. His lectures and writings had a profound influence on modern thought, but as his ideas were popularized they became distorted. It became common to look for hidden symbolic or sexual meaning everywhere.

  A Freudian interpretation is frequently applied to art and can serve to explain the meaning of SYMBOLS and dream or sexual imagery. SURREALIST painters sought to illustrate the unconscious mind in their art and employed symbols described by Freud.

frisket a STENCIL. Available in many forms, frisket paper is used with AIRBRUSH, and a liquid frisket is often used with watercolor.

frontal a point of view in which the represented objects are shown directly facing the viewer. Objects are placed parallel to the picture plane rather than receding in space. A frontal presentation tends to flatten the

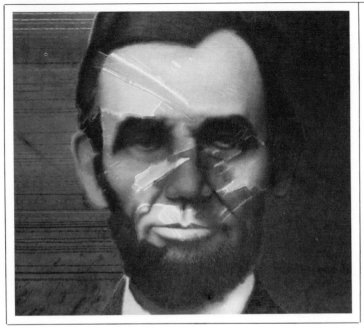

FIGURE 71 Ed Paschke, *Anesthesio*, 1987, oil on linen, 68 × 80″. Courtesy of the Phyllis Kind Gallery—Chicago/New York. Photo by William H. Bengtson.

power and called for the destruction of the art forms of the past. Visual artists responded with their own manifesto, demanding new subject matter which would effectively address the drama of a modern industrialized urban environment. They called for all to join them in the search for an art of new immediacy and intensity which would trigger dynamic sensations of light, color, and sound. Foremost among the Futurists were Umberto Boccioni (Figure 72), Giacomo Balla, and Gino Severini.

genre painting painting representing everyday life and activities. The nineteenth-century academies considered it a distinct category of painting, like landscape or portraiture.

geometric primarily angular in appearance; having reference to simple geometric forms such as circles, triangles, rectangles, or other regular shapes or angles. Geometric is often contrasted with ORGANIC.

geometric harmony a color harmony which results from overlapping a color wheel with a regular polygon (triangle, square, pentagon, hexagon, etc.) and building a composition of the hues indicated by the points of the shape. Geometric harmonies include TRIADIC HARMONY, QUADRATIC HARMONY, and so on (Figure 73).

image, as in Ed Paschke's portrait of Lincoln (Figure 71).

Futurism an Italian movement, 1909–1914, which focused on subjects of the industrial age, science, mechanical power, and urban life. Futurism was influenced by the brilliant color and separated brushstrokes of NEO-IMPRESSIONISM, the faceted forms of CUBISM, and the stop-action effects of sequential high-speed photography. The movement was launched by a literary manifesto which glorified brute

FIGURE 72 Umberto Boccioni, *The City Rises*, 1910, oil on canvas, 6′ 6½″ × 9′ 10½″. Collection, The Museum of Modern Art, New York. Mrs. Simon Guggenheim Fund.

FIGURE 73 Geometric harmonies.

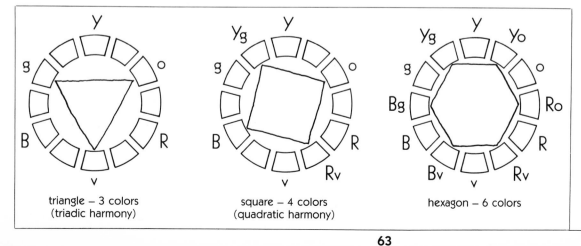

triangle – 3 colors
(triadic harmony)

square – 4 colors
(quadratic harmony)

hexagon – 6 colors

gesso a white GROUND used for painting or for drawing with SILVERPOINT. Traditionally, gesso was a combination of glue and powdered plaster and was used to prepare wooden panels for painting. In contemporary times it most often refers to an acrylic POLYMER-based primer which is used to prepare canvas. The function of gesso is to seal and stabilize the SUPPORT and to provide a uniform painting surface.

Gestalt psychology a school or branch of psychology developed in the 1920s and 1930s. *Gestalt* is a German word meaning "form" or "structure." Gestalt psychology holds that patterns can only be understood as unified wholes and that the whole cannot be understood solely by examining the parts of which it is composed. The belief that a whole is greater than the sum of its parts is at the core of Gestalt psychology.

The Gestalt psychologists were particularly interested in visual perception and sought to understand the means by which FIGURE/GROUND relationships are deciphered. A distinction is drawn between those events which are attended to, the perceptual foreground, and their environment, the perceptual background. Gestalt thinking explores the means by which we distinguish subject from background in perceptual experience.

A fundamental principle of Gestalt psychology states that we will perceive as complete an image as possible, simplifying a complex pattern of multiple parts in order to deal with it as a unified whole. For example, a dotted line is understood as a line, not as a row of independent and unrelated dots.

Artists are particularly interested in Gestalt psychology as it offers a model for understanding the mental process of forming patterns and translating two-dimensional patterns into recognizable images.

gesture refers to the expressive and evocative qualities of an image. A gestural line or stroke conveys the intensity of its creation and makes a direct reference to the movement, pressure, and deliberateness of the drawing or painting process. Gesture is expressive of the artist's relationship to both subject and medium, and captures and reveals the quality of a moment. Spontaneous gesture can be EXPRESSIONISTIC, conveying an immediate and intuitive manner of working, while a more contained gesture suggests a staid, methodical approach.

Both Willem de Kooning (Figure 7) and Jackson Pollock (Figure 11) are described as gestural painters. Their works convey an intense personal involvement in the painting PROCESS and have a freedom and breadth that conveys to the viewer the urgency with which the paint was applied to canvas. A strong directional gesture can be seen in Figure 74, where the boldness of the brushstrokes reinforces the urgency of the figure's movement.

gesture drawing a manner of drawing in which the artist seeks to capture the activity of the model. In contrast to CONTOUR DRAWING, where the lines carefully follow the edges of forms, the lines in a gesture drawing are animated and track the AXIS of the form. Gesture drawings may have a scribbled appearance

FIGURE 74 Robert Barnes, *A Ragno*, 1977, casein on board, 17 × 16″. Courtesy of Struve Gallery, Chicago.

resulting from the artist's concentration on rendering the dynamic qualities of a figure in action, its weight and movement, rather than its strict visual appearance (Figure 75).

golden mean a proportional relationship between two elements where A/B = B/A + B. This ratio is .618 to 1, or approximately 5 to 8. The golden mean, or golden section as it is sometimes known, was recognized in antiquity as an ideal standard of proportions. Proportional relationships corresponding to the golden mean are found throughout nature as well as in many works of art and architecture (Figure 76).

gouache opaque WATERCOLOR, made by the addition of whiting or clay to the pigments.

FIGURE 75 Gwen Knight, *Figure Study #1*, ink and brush, 30 × 22". Courtesy of Francine Seders Gallery, Seattle. Photo by Chris Eden.

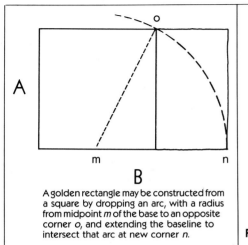

A golden rectangle may be constructed from a square by dropping an arc, with a radius from midpoint *m* of the base to an opposite corner *o*, and extending the baseline to intersect that arc at new corner *n*.

FIGURE 76 A golden rectangle.

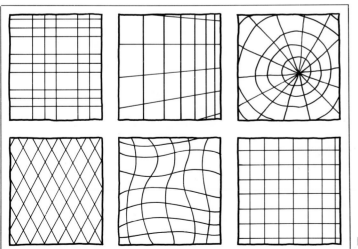

FIGURE 77 Various grids.

graphite   a greasy, dark-gray form of carbon. Graphite is mixed with clay to make the "lead" of pencils. Powdered graphite may also be used as a dry pigment or in paints.

gray scale   see *value scale*

grid   a pattern which divides a pictorial format with crossing lines. Grids are usually formed from horizontal and vertical lines, but many variations are possible (Figure 77). A grid can provide an underlying structure for the organization of a complex visual image, as in Mark Tobey's painting (Figure 14). In addition, a grid may reinforce the rectangularity of the format or

provide a backdrop in front of which the image is organized, as in Jim Nutt's painting *Another Mistake* (Figure 30) or Keith Vaughan's *Blue Figure* (Figure 78).

ground   the base or surface upon which a painting or drawing is made (e.g., GESSO, raw canvas, paper). The choice of ground affects the working characteristics of the MEDIUM and the visual texture of the finished piece.

grouping   principles   those   principles   called   by GESTALT psychologists *Pragnanz*, or "unit-forming" principles, which describe the ways the mind simplifies visual arrays by gathering them into units. When confronted with a complex situation, composed of many parts, the mind seeks to simplify the task of understanding the situation by gathering the parts into groups. Just as when watching a football game we do not attend to twenty-two individual players, but rather to simpler groups like offense and defense or backfield and line, so also in looking at art do we make an effort to gather discrete visual parts into more coherent wholes.

The fundamental grouping principles are *proximity* and *similarity*. We tend to relate objects to one another based on their shared visual characteristics or their relative placement within an image.

FIGURE 78 Keith Vaughn, *Blue Figure*, 1950 gouache on paper, 21½ × 15″. Courtesy of Austin/Desmond Fine Art.

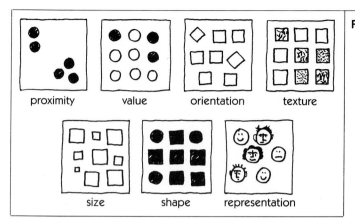

FIGURE 79 Grouping principles.

proximity   value   orientation   texture

size   shape   representation

In our efforts to make sense out of complex visual images, we seek similarities in the visual characteristics of various components of an image. Elements may be grouped by similarities in HUE, VALUE, INTENSITY, SHAPE, size, texture, or orientation. In addition, elements may be grouped by similarity of representation (Figure 79).

harmony   the relationship between two parts of an image. In visual art, as in music, harmony describes relationships between events and is the result of intervals or degrees of contrast. Harmonies most often describe color relationships (see *analogous harmony*; *complementary harmony*; *geometric harmony*), and just as music requires at least two notes sounding simultaneously for there to be harmony, so visual art requires at least two colors or other stimuli. Harmonies result from intervals, distances, and contrasts.

Henri Matisse (Figure 80) was a master at creating harmony through the interplay of color and form, and shape and contour.

hatching   see *cross-hatching*

hot press   a method of making paper or board by subjecting it to extreme pressure and steam, yielding an especially smooth or slick surface sometimes referred to as "plate" or "high" surface. Hot-press papers are less absorbent and have less tooth, or texture, than COLD-PRESS papers.

hue   color. Hue is the dimension of a COLOR which describes its location on the circumference of the COLOR WHEEL. Hue is distinct from VALUE, which describes the lightness or darkness of a color, and INTENSITY, which describes its saturation. Pink and red have the same hue, as do orange and rust or yellow

FIGURE 80 Henry Matisse, *Bathers by a River*, 1916-1917, oil on canvas, 103 × 154″ (259.7 × 389.9 cm). The Art Institute of Chicago, Charles H. and Mary F. S. Worcester Collection, 1953.158. © 1988 The Art Institute of Chicago. All Rights Reserved.

and butterscotch. Hues are described as red, yellow, blue, orange, green, purple, or some combination, such as blue-green.

Brown is not a hue; neither is olive-green. Brown and olive-green describe hues at reduced intensity. Brown is a low-intensity yellow or yellow-orange, and olive-green is a low-intensity yellow-green. Hue refers to a color's location on the circumference of the color wheel, independent of its INTENSITY OR VALUE.

iconic having symbolic CONTENT or meaning. Iconic images convey meaning through explicit SYMBOLS which are understood by the artist. They often rely on conventionalized symbols which are intended to impart specific meaning to the viewer.

iconography the study of the total meaning of a work of art. Iconography goes beyond the subject matter of an art object, considering it within its total cultural context and examining it as an expression of the world view of its maker. Iconography is the study of the FORM and CONTENT of a work of art and how the formal qualities combine to convey meaning.

Traditionally, especially with religious art, iconography has been concerned with the interpretation of SYMBOLS which conveyed specific meanings in particular times and places, even though those meanings may since have been altered or eradicated.

ideation in creativity theory, the process of generating ideas; brainstorming.

illustration an image used primarily to illuminate, convey information about, or draw attention to a subject apart from the image itself. The key distinction between illustration and fine art is the manner in which it is used.

When a tobacco company used Rembrandt's *The Syndics of the Cloth Guild* as part of the trademark for Dutch Masters cigars, they used the painting as an illustration. Larry Rivers's work (Figure 81), with the APPROPRIATED image of the cigar box, stands alone and is not an illustration.

FIGURE 81 Larry Rivers, *Dutch Masters I*, 1963, oil on canvas, 40 × 50″. The Cheekwood Fine Arts Center, Purchased with funds from the National Endowment for the Arts, a federal agency, and matching funds from local donors.

illustration board art paper mounted on a stiff core, usually layered cardboard. Illustration board is widely used in commercial art but may not be suitable for permanent images because of the acid content of the underlying cardboard.

imagery those figures, objects, or things which are the focus of attention within a picture; what is depicted. The imagery an artist employs can be a unifying factor in his or her BODY OF WORK.

impasto in painting, a built-up, textural surface created with thickly applied paint. Impasto conveys an awareness of the physical quality of the paint and the hand of the artist. Impasto makes a major contribution to the effectiveness of Jean Dubuffet's *Beige Man* (Figure 82).

Impressionism a late nineteenth-century movement originating in France. Impressionism emphasized the optical appearance of the visible world. Impressionist artists sought to capture fleeting visual sensations and were particularly responsive to light and atmosphere. Their paintings are characterized by broken brushwork, soft forms, and color saturated by light.

Like the Realist painters before them, the Impressionists painted commonplace subjects from their everyday lives and immediate surroundings. The new availability of oil paint in tubes enabled these artists to paint outside, directly from nature. This resulted in a

FIGURE 82 Jean Dubuffet, *(Beige)* *"Portrait Doré,"* 1945, oil on canvas, 21½ × 18⅛". Courtesy of Richard Gray Gallery.

strong emphasis on landscape in their paintings and imbued Impressionist canvases with a freshness and spontaneity that distinguished them from images created entirely in the studio.

Among the artists associated with Impressionism are Edgar Degas, Claude Monet (Figure 83), Berthe Morrisot, Camille Pissarro, Auguste Renoir, and Alfred Sisley (see also *Realism*).

FIGURE 83 Claude Monet, *On the Seine at Bennecourt (Au Bord de l'eau, Bennecourt)*, 1868, oil on canvas, 31⅞ × 39½″ (81.5 × 100.7 cm). The Art Institute of Chicago, Potter Palmer Collection, 1922.427. © 1988 The Art Institute of Chicago. All Rights Reserved.

FIGURE 84 Paul Wonnar, *Imaginary Still Life with Slice of Cheese*, 1977, acrylic on canvas, 70 × 48″. Collection of Mr. and Mrs. John Berggruen, San Francisco.

informal balance approximate BALANCE achieved by the placement of objects of similar visual weight in arrays that approximate SYMMETRY but are not symmetrical. Paul Wonner's still life (Figure 84) is an extreme example of informal balance. The objects are distributed about a central point, the plum, with a sense of almost equal weight. This radial organization contributes to a general sense of unease in the picture, as it causes us to seek balance not only across the vertical axis, but along the whole array of diagonals as well.

intaglio the family of PRINTMAKING techniques in which the image to be reproduced is cut into the plate. In order to print, the plate is inked and the surface is then wiped clean, leaving ink in the cuts. The press forces the paper into the cuts to pick up the ink. Common intaglio techniques are DRYPOINT, ENGRAVING, and ETCHING.

intensity the dimension of color that measures the brilliance, saturation, or colorfulness of a HUE. The closer a color is to its pure state, the higher its intensity. The lower the amount of hue in a color (the closer it is to gray), the lower its intensity. In mixing colors, either additively or subtractively, intensity is reduced by mixing a hue with its COMPLEMENT.

Intensity can confuse our perception of VALUE. The brightness of a high-intensity, NORMAL VALUE red, blue, or purple may suggest that it is lighter or higher in value than a low-intensity brown of the same value (Figure 85). Intensity is sometimes referred to as *chroma* or *saturation*.

isometric perspective a form of PERSPECTIVE drawing in which parallel lines receding into space do not converge at a vanishing point, but remain parallel. Additionally, proportional relationships between line lengths are maintained. Isometric perspective is used most frequently by engineers and architects to create "measured perspective." In this case, it resembles TWO-POINT PERSPECTIVE, with the receding base lines always at a thirty-degree angle to the horizontal (Figure 86).

Isometric perspective is sometimes referred to as oriental perspective, because traditional methods of drawing in Asia do not use the Renaissance model of LINEAR PERSPECTIVE. Isometric perspective is used occasionally by contemporary artists seeking its distinctive effects.

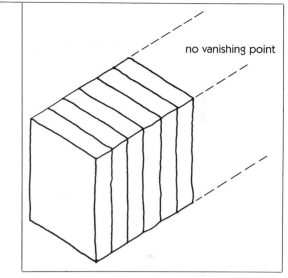

no vanishing point

FIGURE 86 Isometric perspective.

hue	high intensity	low intensity
RED	fire engine	brick
YELLOW	lemon	manila envelope
GREEN	grass	olive

FIGURE 85 Hues at high and low intensity.

FIGURE 87 Roy DeForest, *Untitled*, 1977, lithograph on paper, 24 × 30″. Courtesy of Struve Gallery, Chicago.

Jugendstil   German for "youth style." A German variant of ART NOUVEAU.

Jungian   pertaining to the theories of Carl Gustav Jung. After studying with Sigmund FREUD, Jung developed an understanding of personality shaped by two components: the personal incidents of an individual's life and the submerged historical memory of all peoples, which he called the collective unconscious. In the 1930s, artists responded to Jung's writings and were struck by his emphasis on myth and archetypes, symbols which originate in the collective unconscious and transcend a single time or culture. Jung's theories held significance for artists active in the later years of the SURREALIST movement and for the ABSTRACT EXPRESSIONIST generation.

line   that element of form which is characterized by length and direction. When a line becomes too broad in relation to its length, it begins to assume the characteristics of SHAPE.

Line quality may be widely varied and is responsive to the tool used to make it, the physical GESTURE with which it is drawn, its direction, its texture, and its interaction with adjacent lines and other FORMAL ELEMENTS. Roy DeForest's LITHOGRAPH with the multiple images of a dog (Figure 87) is built from a multitude of linear interactions.

Line may be the sole formal element in a drawing. It may be used as an outline to define CONTOUR or it may be used to model, as in hatching. Line may be thick or thin, soft or hard, flowing or ragged, smooth or irreg-

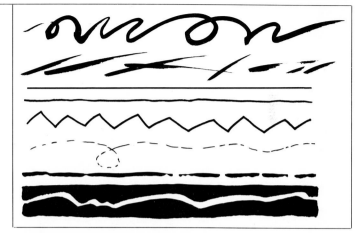

FIGURE 88   Various types of line.

ular. It may be cool and objective or bold and expressive (Figure 88).

linear perspective   a term which describes those methods of creating an illusion of depth, first applied in the Renaissance, which rely on the principle that parallel lines receding into space *appear* to converge at a VANISHING POINT. (See also *one-point perspective*; *two-point perspective*; *three-point perspective*.)

line drawing   drawing which is created exclusively through the use of line, without areas of contrasting

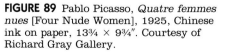

color or value. Pablo Picasso (Figure 89) and David Hockney (Figure 90) are both masters of creating expressive images using line.

line of sight   the implicit line along which the vision of a figure in a painting moves. Just as you will be tempted to look up if you walk into a room where everyone is looking at the ceiling, so an artist can direct our attention within a picture by directing the attention of the figures within the image. Andrew Stevovich uses this device in his painting *At the Track* (Figure 91) to establish a conceptual FOCAL POINT outside of the physical confines of the picture. This strong directional emphasis is balanced by the backward glance of the figure in the lower right-hand corner, whose eyes turn our attention back into the picture.

FIGURE 89 Pablo Picasso, *Quatre femmes nues* [Four Nude Women], 1925, Chinese ink on paper, 13¾ × 9¾". Courtesy of Richard Gray Gallery.

FIGURE 90 David Hockney, *Frankie, Fire Island*, 1972, ink on paper, 17½ × 13¾″. Courtesy of Richard Gray Gallery.

FIGURE 91 Andrew Stevovich, *At the Track*, 1987, oil on linen, 36 × 42″. Private collection. Photo courtesy of Coe Kerr Gallery, Inc. Photo by Greg Heins.

lithography a printmaking technique which relies on the principle that oil and water do not mix. A lithography plate, traditionally limestone, is highly polished and then drawn on with a grease-based medium in the areas which are to print. The stone is then lightly etched with acid, the grease-based medium serving as a RESIST. The areas which have been drawn upon retain their polish, while the exposed areas of the stone become porous.

During the printing process, the stone is first wetted. Water runs away from the polished areas of the plate just as it runs off a highly waxed car, while the areas of the plate that have been etched hold the water. The oil-based ink, applied with a roller, adheres to the drawn surfaces on the stone (Figure 92).

Maurice Kerrigan's ¿*Snow Dog?* is an example of a lithograph (Figure 93).

FIGURE 92 Steps in the procedure of making a lithograph. Top view and exaggerated cross section of stone.

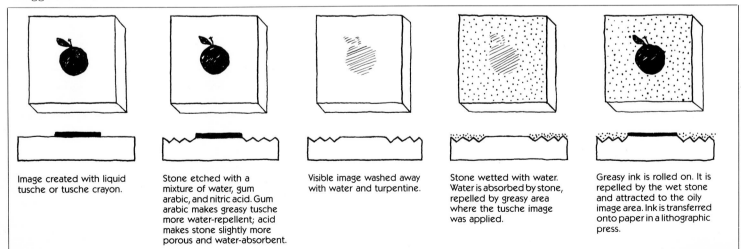

Image created with liquid tusche or tusche crayon.

Stone etched with a mixture of water, gum arabic, and nitric acid. Gum arabic makes greasy tusche more water-repellent; acid makes stone slightly more porous and water-absorbent.

Visible image washed away with water and turpentine.

Stone wetted with water. Water is absorbed by stone, repelled by greasy area where the tusche image was applied.

Greasy ink is rolled on. It is repelled by the wet stone and attracted to the oily image area. Ink is transferred onto paper in a lithographic press.

FIGURE 93 Maurie Kerrigan, *¿Snow Dog?*, 1982, lithograph, 22 × 30". Private Collection.

local color the actual color of an object in normal daylight, as opposed to PERCEIVED COLOR. For example, the local color of a white house is always white; seen at sunset, it might appear red or purple.

mat a protective frame made from a quality cardboard. A mat serves two functions. First, it visually completes an image, separating it from the outside world and providing a bridge between objective reality and the work of art itself. As such, a mat should be unobtrusive and neutral in color. A highly colored mat has an active effect upon the artwork and its surroundings and detracts from the strength of the work.

Second, a mat protects the surface of a work on paper by creating a raised border around it. If framed under glass, the mat serves to lift the glass off of the artwork.

There are many ways to construct a mat, but one of the most professional is a hinged mat (Figure 94), which provides a rigid back for the artwork, easy access to the image, and requires a minimum of attachment to the artwork itself. Mats and backings should be made from high-quality, acid-free board to protect the artwork from oxidation.

measured perspective   see *isometric perspective*

media   plural of MEDIUM

FIGURE 94 Hinged mat.

medium   (1) the general technique or method by which an image or art object is made; for example, PAINTING, DRAWING, or ENGRAVING. In this usage the plural form is *media*.

(2) the specific material or technique used in the making of an image or art object; for example, WATERCOLOR, colored-pencil, CONTÉ CRAYON, or GRAPHITE. In this usage the plural form is *media*.

(3) the specific recipe or mixture of BINDERS and solvents used to thin and extend paint and to control its manipulative qualities. In this usage the plural form is *mediums*.

metamorphosis   a change from one formal configuration into another. In art and design, metamorphosis emphasizes the process of change and the intermediate or transitional stages between two formal states.

Minimal Art   a movement which originated in the early 1960s and stressed a simple, direct expression of materials. Minimal Art is self-referential in that it emphasizes the visual sensation of the image itself, outside of any representational or metaphorical associations. It is reductivist in its disciplined organization of a small set of FORMAL elements. Minimalist paintings generally offer broad expanses of flat color with limited juxtapositions of FORM or color contrasts, avoiding any suggestion of illusion or representation of the external world. They are impersonal in execution, simple, and objectlike.

Leading Minimalist painters include Ellsworth Kelly (Figure 95), Brice Marden, and Frank Stella.

modeling the use of value gradation to suggest the illusion of solidness. Modeling may be arbitrary and done in a manner that does not mimic nature, as in the work of Fernand Leger (Figure 96) and Roger Brown (Figure 13), or naturalistic, as in James Valerio's *Dishes*

FIGURE 95 Ellsworth Kelly, *Running White*, 1959, oil on canvas, 7′4″ × 68″. Collection, The Museum of Modern Art, New York. Purchase.

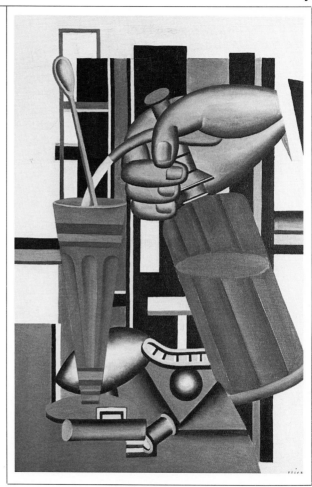

FIGURE 96 Fernand Leger, *Le Siphon*, [The Siphon], 1924, oil on canvas, 36 × 23⅝″. Courtesy of Richard Gray Gallery.

FIGURE 97 James Valerio, *Dishes*, 1984, graphite on paper, 30 × 40″. Courtesy of Struve Gallery, Chicago.

FIGURE 98 Alfredo Arraguin, *Tapete*, 1983, oil on canvas, 84 × 60″. Courtesy of Foster/White Gallery, Seattle.

(Figure 97). The Leger painting shows a variety of approaches to modeling, from the formulaic treatment of the hand to the more conventional treatment of the spoon.

modern art art of the late nineteenth and twentieth centuries. In its most narrow usage, the term *modern art* refers only to art created between 1880 and 1945, from POST-IMPRESSIONISM to ABSTRACT EXPRESSIONISM, but in common usage it refers also to CONTEMPORARY ART.

module a visual unit used repetitively as a "building block" to create a PATTERN or total visual structure. Alfredo Arreguin uses a modular approach in developing his images (Figures 98 and 99). While one conforms to a rigid geometric GRID structure, the other is more fluidly organized with a greater variety of modules.

FIGURE 99 Alfredo Arraguin, *Confetti*, 1986, oil on canvas, 60 × 48″. Courtesy of Foster/White Gallery, Seattle.

monochromatic composed of a single HUE. A monochromatic image is one made using only colors of the same hue. Variety may be introduced only by variations in VALUE and INTENSITY.

monotype a unique print made by painting or drawing directly on the plate. Because the image is not a part of the plate, it changes every time a print is made. Monotype combines the immediacy and uniqueness of painting with the FLAT surface quality of a print.

motif a distinct GESTURE, FORM, PATTERN, IMAGE, or subject, repeated in an individual work or throughout a BODY OF WORK. Mark Rothko's hovering rectangles (Figure 6) are a motif which provides a visual and thematic link throughout his mature works. Roger Brown makes pronounced use of repeated motifs including silhouetted figures and striated clouds in his work (Figure 11).

FIGURE 100 Ken Holder, *Drifter #8*,
1987, acrylic on canvas, 49 × 158″.
Courtesy of the artist.

movement a discernible trend or direction in art, characterized by a shared body of thought and often by shared stylistic tendencies. A particular STYLE or set of visual characteristics may typify a movement, but style alone is not enough to define a movement. Like political movements, art movements exist in a discrete period of time and are founded on conceptual issues.

multiple format a pictorial organization which combines two or more distinct compositions, with clearly defined borders or limits, to create a total image. The simplest forms of multiple FORMAT are the DIPTYCH and TRIPTYCH.

Ken Holder's painting (Figure 100) is much more complex and reveals various ways in which the juxtaposition of multiple formats can become a dominant factor in the organization of works of art.

multiple point of view   the depiction of a scene from several points of view within a single image. Mike Hascall (Figure 101) makes use of multiple points of view to present an image of a car driving along a mountain road at night. David Hockney also employs multiple points of view in his photocollages composed of Polaroid photos shot from multiple vantage points (Figure 102).

Munsell system   a system of color notation devised by Albert F. Munsell. The system was first proposed in 1915 and defines color in terms of HUE, VALUE, and chroma (INTENSITY).

FIGURE 101 Mike Hascall, *Night Arrangement*, 1986, acrylic on canvas, 104 × 84″. Courtesy of Linda Farris Gallery, Seattle.

FIGURE 102 David Hockney, *Ian Washing His Hair*, 1983, photographic collage, ed. 6/15, 30 × 33″. Courtesy of Richard Gray Gallery.

mural a large painting or drawing created on or mounted flush with an interior or exterior wall. A mural is often integrated with and responsive to the architectural structure where it is situated.

Because of their size and location and their ability to address a large audience murals have often been vehicles for the expression of political, social, and cultural beliefs. In this century American painters active with the Works Progress Administration during the depression era and Mexican painters active in the 1920s and 1930s saw mural painting as a means of inspiring the public, propagandizing achievements, and warning of ideological and philosophical threats to the common good.

Nabis, Les from the Hebrew word meaning "prophet." Les Nabis were a group of young French artists, including Maurice Denis, Paul Serusier, Pierre Bonnard, and Edouard Vuillard, who were greatly attracted to the POST-IMPRESSIONIST painter Paul Gauguin. Gauguin's paintings, which had strong DECORATIVE qualities resulting from his use of bold flat colors, impressed Les Nabis as an alternative to the NATURALISM of earlier IMPRESSIONISM. The emphasis in many paintings by Les Nabis is on subject matter which is ambiguous or nonspecific places their work within the SYMBOLIST movement.

naive art the art of the untrained or untutored. "Naive" is used to describe the art of children or adults who have not received significant instruction in the visual arts.

Throughout the twentieth century, works by naive artists have been praised for their directness of approach and freedom from ACADEMIC mannerisms. Many sophisticated artists, including Jean Dubuffet (Figure 103) and Gaylen Hansen (Figure 139) have responded to the freshness and vitality of naive art and have welcomed its influence in their own paintings.

FIGURE 103 Jean Dubuffet, *Site Avec Quinze Personnages* [Site with Fifteen Personages], 1980, ink on paper with collage, 20 × 13¾". Courtesy of Richard Gray Gallery.

narrative art art which suggests or tells a story. Narrative art uses recognizable imagery to present the outlines of an event. As such, it involves the intellect of the viewer in a response not only to the appearance of the image, its STYLE, COMPOSITION, and FORMAL characteristics, but also to the events depicted and the possibilities which might precede or follow them. Narrative is a major element in the work of Michael Ehle (Figure 104) and Roger Brown (Figure 13).

naturalism an attitude towards representation which involves the rendering of nature in a straightforward way, responsive to the perceived world. Naturalism is a realistic approach to artmaking and has been the dominant tendency throughout much of the history of Western art. While naturalism and realism are often used interchangeably, the term should not be used to define the nineteenth-century movement REALISM.

negative shape shape created in the background of an image by the interaction of the CONTOURS of the POSITIVE SHAPES and the edge of the format. TENSION can be introduced into an image by balancing the interest of the positive and negative shapes. In *Large Bird, Flushed* (Figure 105), Tony Phillips aggressively creates negative shapes by his placement of the bird with its contours joining the border on three sides and overlapping the tree at the bottom of the picture (Figure 106).

Neo-Expressionism a revival, first evidenced in the mid-1970s, of early twentieth-century tendencies toward intense color, bold distortions, and gestural brushwork. (See also *expressionistic*.)

FIGURE 104 Michael Ehle, *Tango Toro*, 1986, gouache on ricepaper, 36 × 24″. Courtesy of Greg Kucera, Gallery, Seattle.

FIGURE 105 Tony Phillips, *Large Bird, Flushed*, 1981, charcoal, 22 × 30".
Courtesy of Marianne Deson Gallery.

FIGURE 106 Negative shapes from Tony Phillips's drawing.

FIGURE 107 Georges Seurat, *A Sunday
Afternoon on the Island of the Grande
Jatte*, 1884-1886, oil on canvas, 81 ×
120⅜″ (207.6 × 308.0 cm). The Art
Institute of Chicago, Helen Birch Bartlett
Memorial Collection, 1926.224. © 1988
The Art Institute of Chicago. All Rights
Reserved.

Neo-Impressionism the term used to describe the stylistic tendencies of Georges Seurat (Figure 107) and his followers. Neo-Impressionist painters pursued IMPRESSIONIST subjects including landscape and urban life. The light, airy color of their paintings is indebted to Impressionism as well. Seurat felt Impressionism to be too fleeting; suggestive of only a moment in time. In his own work, he sought effects of monumentality and timelessness. He was particularly interested in the new scientific theories regarding color and perception, and he applied these theories to his paintings, in part as a reaction against the more intuitive and casual use of color by the Impressionists. Seurat's paintings, as those of his followers, are characterized by POINTILLIST (divisionist) brushstrokes and rigidly structured compositions.

In addition to Seurat, artists associated with Neo-Impressionism include Henri-Edmund Cross and Paul Signac.

neutral color a color of low INTENSITY, such as beige, olive, rust, or mauve. In the COLOR WHEEL, neutral colors will be found at the hub, around the central gray (Figure 108). They are made by mixing a HUE with its COMPLEMENT or gray. Because they are composed of a balanced range of hues, neutral colors contrast less than colors of higher intensity and are therefore useful in unifying the color scheme of a composition.

newsprint a relatively inexpensive, off-white paper made from wood pulp and recycled paper. Newsprint is available with a rough or smooth surface and is attractive for studies and sketches because of its affor-

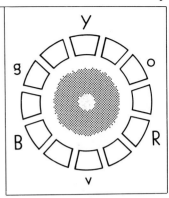

FIGURE 108 Location of neutral colors on a color wheel.

dability. Due to its high acid content, newsprint is not a stable paper and will yellow and become brittle over time.

nonobjective not referring to objects. Nonobjective images do not represent objects or things. They are not abstractions of the seen world.

Nonobjective art is constructed solely through the interaction of FORMAL elements. It emerged during the 1910s as an effort on the part of artists to create a purely visual art free from direct representation of the external world. (See also *abstract*.)

nonrepresentational see *nonobjective*

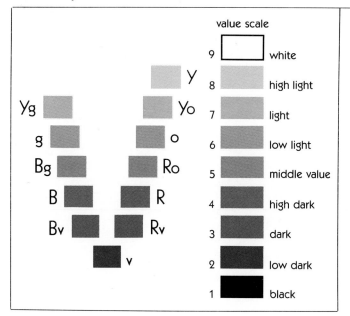

value scale

9	white
8	high light
7	light
6	low light
5	middle value
4	high dark
3	dark
2	low dark
1	black

FIGURE 109 Normal values of hues.

normal value   the VALUE of a HUE at its highest INTENSITY. The normal value of yellow is relatively high, while the normal value of blue is relatively low (Figure 109).

objective color   see *local color*

objective drawing   drawing which represents and records the world as seen, without DISTORTION. In objective drawing there is an effort to maintain a point-for-point correlation between an existent external reality and the work of the artist.

oblique perspective   see *isometric perspective*

oil paint   paint which uses a vegetable-based drying oil, usually linseed oil, as a BINDER for the PIGMENT. In addition to pigment and oil, oil paints may include additional agents to control drying. Among the advantages of working in oils is that the colors do not change upon drying.

Another quality of oil-based paints is that the MEDIUM does not cause vegetable fibers to swell and shrink, so oil media can be used on paper GROUNDS without concerns of warping the surface. The oil medium will, however, penetrate the fibers of the paper, and there is danger of rotting if the SUPPORT is not properly prepared.

oil pastel   a drawing material in which the PIGMENT is bound with a mixture of oil and wax, sometimes called craypas.

one-point perspective   a system of LINEAR PERSPECTIVE which allows representation of rectangular solids oriented frontally, parallel and perpendicular to

FIGURE 110 Susan Kraut, *Two Tables with City Skyline*, 1979, oil on canvas, 30 × 42″. Courtesy of Marianne Deson Gallery.

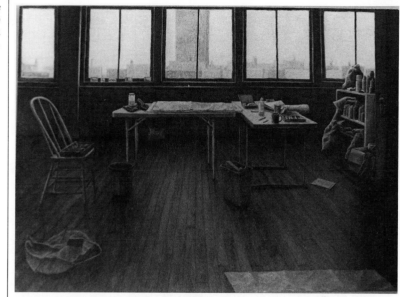

FIGURE 111 Illustration of one-point perspective Susan Kraut's painting.

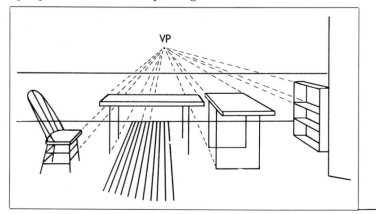

the PICTURE PLANE. One vanishing point is established at the horizon for all lines or edges which are receding in space, the ORTHOGONALS. Lines which are parallel to the viewer do not recede in space and so do not converge at a vanishing point.

Susan Kraut's depiction of a studio interior (Figure 110) is built on one-point perspective. The perspective is revealed by the orthogonal lines of the floorboards, the edges of the tables, and the bookshelves all converging at a single vanishing point (Figure 111).

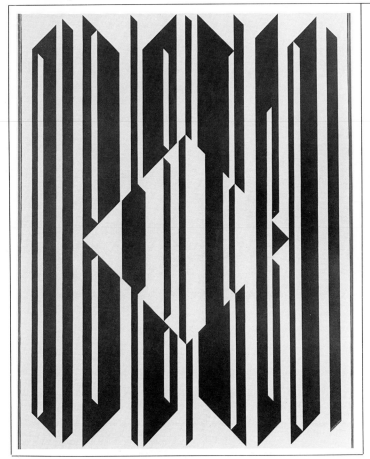

FIGURE 112 Victor Vasarely, *Leyre*,
n. d., oil on canvas, 51 × 38″. Krannert
Art Museum, University of Illinois,
Urbana-Champaign.

Op Art   short for "optical" art. A movement originating in the mid-1960s in which perceptual shifts and ambiguities, such as illusions of depth or movement, are stressed. Op paintings trick the viewer into sensing motion or flux within the patterns of a flat, painted surface by presenting tightly rendered patterns and the vibration of color contrasts.

   Among the major Op painters are Bridget Riley and Victor Vasarely (Figure 112).

optical color   see *perceived color*

organic   an adjective used to describe abstract forms which are evocative of the world of nature. Organic imagery is usually characterized by flowing lines and rounded shapes. Organic forms are often contrasted with GEOMETRIC forms, as in the work of Barbara Rossi (Figure 113).

oriental perspective   see *isometric perspective*

orthogonals   in ONE-POINT PERSPECTIVE, the lines perpendicular to the PICTURE PLANE, receding into space towards the vanishing point.

overlapping   overlapping occurs when one object or shape in an image passes in front of another, interrupting its CONTOUR. Overlapping is one of the most basic means of creating an illusion of space and defining spatial relationships. It is most effective when the contour of the overlapped shape is broken aggressively. If the contours align, we may perceive the objects as adjacent to one another rather than in front or behind (Figure 114).

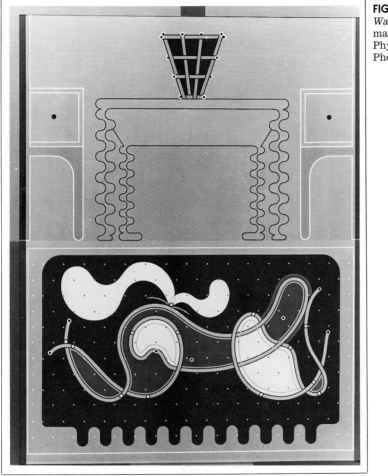

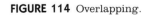

FIGURE 113 Barbara Rossi, *A Lady Waiting for Dinner*, 1983, acrylic on masonite, 45 × 35⅞". Courtesy of the Phyllis Kind Gallery—Chicago/New York. Photo by William H. Bengtson.

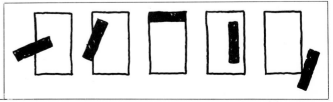

FIGURE 114 Overlapping.

FIGURE 115 William Conger, *Aurea*, 1980, oil on linen, 48 × 46″. Courtesy of Roy Boyd Gallery, Chicago.

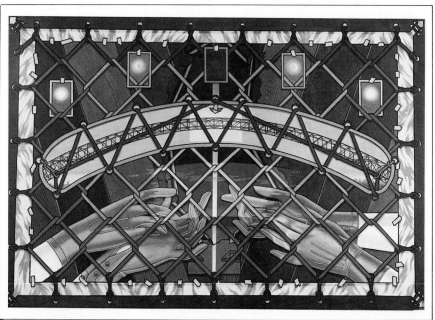

FIGURE 116 Art Green, *Agreeable Fiction*, 1976, oil on canvas, 48 × 72″. Courtesy of the Phyllis Kind Gallery—Chicago/New York. Photo by William H. Bengtson.

FIGURE 117 Wesley Kimler, *Acteon*, 1986, oil on canvas, 86 × 76″. Courtesy of Struve Gallery, Chicago.

The primary spatial device used in both William Conger's and Art Green's paintings (Figures 115 and 116) is overlapping. (See also *shared contour*.)

painterly suggestive of the loose, fluid qualities and pronounced brushwork unique to painting media. Painterly works reveal the artist's sense of touch and evoke the physical PROCESS of painting. The visual TEXTURE of the image often contributes to the painterly quality of a work. Painterly work is generally composed of broad rather than linear activity. Wesley Kimler's *Actaeon* (Figure 117) displays painterly qualities through gestural brushstrokes and the emphasis on the liquid quality of the paint.

painting the process of creating images from a material composed of PIGMENT mixed with and suspended in a relatively fluid medium such as oil, acrylic resin, glue, egg yolk, melted wax, or water.

Paintings are generally defined by the interaction of broad areas of color rather than lines. Because of this, images created with PASTELS are often referred to as "pastel paintings".

paper a flexible material in sheet form made from matted and intertwined fibers. Paper is generally made from plant materials and is held together by the interlocking of the individual fibers rather than by an adhesive bonding agent. Papers may be treated with a chemical sizing agent to provide them with additional stiffness and stability. In addition, they may be subjected to pressure or run through rollers to control their surface texture. The working qualities of a paper are determined by the fiber of which it is composed and the manner in which it is formed.

When using water-based media on paper, care must be taken to avoid warpage resulting from the absorbtion of water into the fibers. This warpage is not a problem when using oil-based media on paper.

parallel perspective   see *one-point perspective*

pastel   (1) powdered pigments blended with a BINDER and CHALK and pressed into stick form. The hardness of pastels is controlled by the amount of binder used. Chalk is added to the pigment to control the depth of the color. Images created with pastels straddle the line between DRAWING and PAINTING. They can combine the dry and linear character of drawing with the blending of broad areas of color associated with painting.

(2) pale colors, such as pink or powder blue are TINTS of HUES at high VALUE and INTENSITY and are often referred to as pastel shades.

Pattern painting   a tendency first evidenced in the mid-1970s toward highly active, DECORATIVE paintings which frequently involve an eclectic combination of colorful designs and MOTIFS. Many of the Pattern painters emphasize deliberately crude, emblematic patterns, brilliant colors, and fanciful combinations of surface TEXTURE, often incorporating textiles with colors and designs which interact discordantly.

Among the major Pattern Painters are Kim Mac-Connel (Figure 118) and Robert Kushner.

perceived color   the sensed color of an object. Perceived color is a result of the interaction of the eye and mind with the LOCAL COLOR of an object, light reflected from that object, and any intervening medium which filters or modifies that reflected light. For example, a white house seen at sunset or through a red filter might appear to be red or pink. While its local color is white, its perceived color is altered by the situation.

Our response to perceived color is relative to context. Although sunglasses shift the HUES of anything seen through them, the mind rapidly adapts, and by interpolation we are still able to distinguish local color with a high degree of precision. (See also *film color*; *volume color*.)

permanence   stability and unchangeability. Permanence has long been an issue in the arts. The development of PAINTING media has been driven by a search for PIGMENTS and BINDERS which would remain stable over time, without discoloration or separation from one another or the SUPPORT.

In the twentieth century, permanence has emerged as a philosophical issue as well. The DADA movement gave birth to art that was intentionally temporary. Many artists of the 1950s and 1960s were unconcerned about the permanence of their materials. Their concern was about PROCESS and conceptual issues, not the permanence of the art object. Many experimented with unconventional and previously untried media and methods without concern for the stability of their materials. With the passage of time, difficult problems of conserving these pieces have emerged for museums and collectors. Contemporary artists are increasingly aware of permanence as an issue in their work.

perspective   literally "point of view." In art, perspective

FIGURE 118 Kim MacConnel, *Shakey*, c. 1980-1981, acrylic on cotton, 92 × 116″. Courtesy of Holly Solomon Gallery, New York. Photo by D. James Dee, New York.

refers to some of the devices used to achieve an illusion of space in two-dimensional images. LINEAR PERSPECTIVE refers to drawing systems which represent the perceived diminution in size of objects as they recede into space, while ATMOSPHERIC PERSPECTIVE refers to the perceived effects of atmosphere on color and value.

Photorealism a primarily American art movement of the late 1960s and the '70s, sometimes referred to as *Superrealism*. Photorealism was based on the camera's rendering of the appearance of the external world and was attentive to the decision-making process involved in the translation of photographed imagery to painting. While artists have used photography as a resource from the time of its discovery, the Photorealists were the first to openly and aggressively copy photographic images. Many of the artists painted from slides projected directly onto their canvases and followed the photographic source religiously, mimicking the distortions of color and form inherent in photography.

Although the Photorealists were objective in the rendering of their images, often suspending aesthetic judgments during the actual process of painting, they made initial decisions in the choice of IMAGE, FORMAT, and method of representation, which distinguished their work from simple copying.

The subject matter of most Photorealist paintings is mundane, from Chuck Close's greatly enlarged closeups of ordinary faces to Richard Estes's typical urban environments (Figure 119). In this, the art of the Photorealists has been linked to POP ART, with its emphasis on easily accessible images drawn from everyday life.

The FLAT, impersonal surfaces of photorealist paintings create impact through TROMPE L'OEIL effects which immediately evoke an awareness of the precision and care required in their making. In looking at a Photorealist painting, we are impressed as much by artisanship as by image. The explicit detailing of the paintings provides a profusion of focused detail that corresponds much more to the way in which we see photographs than to the way we are inclined to see the world around us. Just as the camera makes no distinction between what is important or insignificant in recording a scene, so the Photorealists pay equal attention to all parts of their images, creating a visual field in which all parts of the image compete for our attention. For example, Estes's attention to the complex reflections of the chrome surfaces of the telephone booths gives the scene a complexity that we would likely disregard in normal viewing.

Other painters associated with the movement include Robert Bechtel, Audrey Flack, Ralph Goings, and Malcolm Morley.

pictorial space the illusionistic space represented within a picture. The pictorial space of an image is one of the strong controllers of our response to that image. Artists manipulate pictorial space by a number of means including LINEAR PERSPECTIVE, ATMOSPHERIC PERSPECTIVE, and SPATIAL COLOR.

The creation and control of pictorial space has emerged from time to time as a primary focus of artistic attention. In the Renaissance, artists explored linear

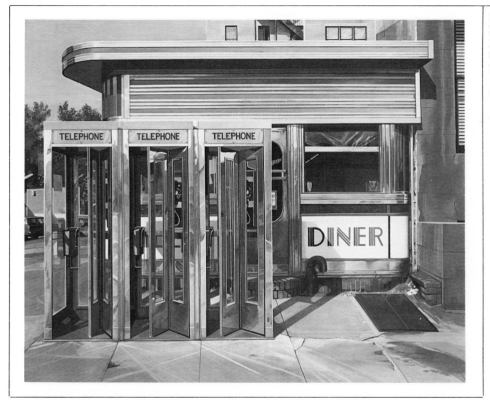

FIGURE 119 Richard Estes, *Diner*, 1971, oil on canvas, 40⅛ × 50″. Hirshhorn Museum and Sculpture Garden, Smithsonian Institution, Purchased from the Allan Stone Gallery, 1977.

perspective as a means of creating a unified pictorial space that conveyed a coherence and depth corresponding closely to human vision. In the nineteenth century, artists such as J. M. W. Turner created tangible pictorial space through the use of atmospheric perspective. In the mid-twentieth century, Hans Hofmann (see cover) and his followers concentrated their attention on the "push and pull" effects of color to create dynamic tensions within a relatively shallow pictorial space. In the 1960s, artists such as Ellsworth Kelly (Figure 95) limited pictorial space by asserting the flatness of the PICTURE PLANE.

FIGURE 120 Richard Hull, *Scaffolds*, 1986, oil and wax on linen, 48 × 60″. Courtesy of the Phyllis Kind Gallery, Chicago/New York. Photo by William H. Bengtson.

Richard Hull uses a variety of approaches to pictorial space in his painting *Scaffolds* (Figure 120), creating a dynamic TENSION between suggestions of depth and assertions of flatness.

picture plane   a sensed invisible plane coincident with the flat surface of a painting or drawing. The sense of the picture plane frequently works in contrast to our sense of PICTORIAL SPACE, creating a tension between the physicality of the flat surface of two-dimensional art and the three-dimensionality of illusionistic space.

pigment   the material which provides color in MEDIA. Pigments are chemical materials ground into fine powders. They may be used directly in their dry form, but are usually mixed with a BINDER to create a material with more controllable working characteristics.

Paints are often named after the pigment from which they are made. Cadmium red and cobalt blue are made from the minerals cadmium and cobalt. EARTH COLORS are so named because their pigments are clays. Burnt sienna and raw sienna were originally made from clay dug in the vicinity of Sienna, Italy, with the earth being used in its charred or "burnt" state in the one, and in its "raw" state in the other.

Modern paints generally list the pigments on the label.

planographic those PRINTMAKING techniques which do not rely on RELIEF, the texture of the printing plate, to distinguish inked from non-inked areas. Planographic techniques include LITHOGRAPHY, MONOTYPE, and SILKSCREEN.

Pointillism term used to describe POST-IMPRESSION-IST paintings by Georges Seurat (Figure 107) and his followers. Pointillism describes the technique of inter-mingling small dabs or dots of relatively high-intensity colors in order to achieve an optical mixture as a result of the BEZOLD EFFECT. This optical mixture is most effective if the viewer is at a distance from the canvas sufficient to allow the individual bits of color to blur and blend. This technique was the result of Seurat's interest in the work of the color theorists of his time, and he called it and its resultant effect of bright, clean, pure color *Divisionism*.

polychromatic multicolored.

polymer medium acrylic polymer used as a MEDIUM for ACRYLIC paints. Polymer medium, available in glossy or matte form and as a liquid or a gel, is used with acrylic paints in much the same way that linseed oil (a natural polymer) is used with oil paints.

polyptych a term used to describe images composed of multiple frames or subformats within a single FOR-MAT. Polyptychs may be composed of physically discrete panels or a single SUPPORT with clearly defined borders between several parts. Roger Brown's painting (Figure 13) is a polyptych on six panels. (See also *diptych*; *triptych*.)

Pop Art a term originally used in the 1950s to describe the work of English artists who were exploring popular culture as a source for their imagery. Pop Art is an American art movement originating in New York City in the early 1960s. Those artists most closely associated with Pop include Andy Warhol (Figure 121), Claes Oldenburg, Roy Lichtenstein, and James Rosenquist.

FIGURE 121 Andy Warhol, *Marilyn*, 1967, silkscreen, 36 × 36 ". Krannert Art Museum, University of Illinois, Urbana-Champaign.

These Pop artists embraced images from the mass media and adopted techniques from the world of commercial art, including the bold graphics of billboard illustrations and the flat, linear, impersonal line of comic strips. Their forays into popular culture resulted in images that were familiar and accessible to the general public. Pop Art is characterized by a sense of humor and even irony in its elevation of mundane objects to the status of high art. This is accomplished by enlarging commonplace objects and images and objectively rendering them in the medium of fine art, paint on canvas. Pop Art's origins lie in the nihilistic works of DADA, which had earlier challenged the boundaries between high art and the visual environment of the everyday world. The cool and emotionally uninvolved handling of the paint in Pop canvases was seen as a reaction against the emotional drama of the ABSTRACT EXPRESSIONIST works of the previous decade.

The New York-based Pop movement sparked an interest in the images of consumer culture among artists throughout the country and artists in areas like Chicago and on the West Coast developed their own distinctive styles.

positive shape   shape seen as FIGURE or foreground. Positive shape refers to those shapes actively produced by the artist. It is contrasted with NEGATIVE SHAPE. (See also *figure/ground*.)

poster paint   an inexpensive, opaque, water-based paint with a glue or gum BINDER.

FIGURE 122 Paul Cezanne, *Pines and Rocks*, c. 1900, oil on canvas, 32 × 25¾". Collection, The Museum of Modern Art. Lillie P. Bliss Collection.

Post-Impressionism   a term coined in 1910 to describe the stylistic tendencies of those artists who pursued unexplored implications of the IMPRESSIONIST movement. Paul Gauguin and Vincent van Gogh employed the heightened color of the Impressionists to evoke intense psychological responses. Paul Cezanne (Figure 122), after exhibiting with the Impressionists, developed a more systematic style of brushwork and more rigidly structured compositions. Georges Seurat (Figure 107) and his followers are also commonly grouped with the Post-Impressionists. (See also *Neo-Impressionism*.)

Post-Modernism   a term first widely used in the late 1970s to describe contemporary developments in architecture, Post-Modernism now refers to tendencies including the layering and discontinuity of meaning in contemporary art. It is characterized by references to the art of the past and questions the possibility of originality and relevance in contemporary art.

Cindy Sherman's photographs, self-portraits in a variety of guises, are typical of Post-Modernism. In (Figures 123 and 124), the artist poses and costumes herself in such a way as to suggest that she is an actor in a NARRATIVE. Drama is implied, but there is no

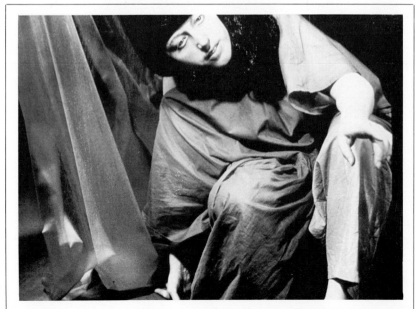

FIGURE 123 Cindy Sherman, *Untitled*, 1983, type "C" print, 30 × 40″. Courtesy of Rhona Hoffman Gallery.

107

FIGURE 124 Cindy Sherman, *Untitled*, 1982, type "C" print, 45 × 30″. Courtesy of Rona Hoffman Gallery.

clear sequence of events. The images have the qualities of a publicity photograph or a "still" from an unknown film of the past. Sherman's methods and procedures in making her images are highly deliberate. While costuming, stance, camera angle, and lighting are carefully planned, the work remains psychologically ambiguous. Visual information, even an excess of information, is provided, but the pictorial and emotional clues do not constitute an expressive whole. Each scene is staged in such a way as to deny a complete and whole understanding. The compelling reality of the photographic image contrasts with the psychological disorientation provoked by the missing links in the implied narrative. Alternate meanings collide, confuse, and subvert one another.

The APPROPRIATION of imagery is a distinguishing characteristic of Post-Modernism. Sherrie Levine's appropriation of Walker Evans's photograph (Figure 17) raises questions about the idea of the "masterpiece." The meaning of David Salle's painting *Footmen* (Figure 58) is clouded by the appropriation of a grinning face from a painting by the seventeenth-century master Diego Velasquez and the juxtaposition of seemingly unrelated images. To understand the significance of this act of appropriation, it must be realized that Salle makes frequent use of imagery appropriated from the realm of high art as well as from popular culture—cartoon images for example. With Levine and Salle, appropriation becomes an issue in and of itself, an issue which contributes to but does not explain the full meaning of the resultant image.

FIGURE 125 Charles Sheeler, *American Landscape*, 1930, oil on canvas, 24 × 31″. Collection, The Museum of Modern Art, New York. Gift of Abby Aldrich Rockefeller.

Post-Modernism has been described as heralding the end of the modernist notion of an AVANT-GARDE. The experiment and risk which characterized modern art movements and distinguished individual avant-garde artists such as Marcel Duchamp and Pablo Picasso as champions of the "new" is subverted by the Post-Modernists' return to and revision of styles and mannerisms of the past. The willful eclecticism of Post-Modern artists, with their dependence on the forms and images of the past emptied of their original CONTENT and their intentional layering and confusion of meaning, is indicative of nihilism. Underlying their work is the suggestion that contemporary art is incapable of provoking truly new and fresh responses.

Precisionism a movement of the late 1920s and '30s in American painting and photography, in which artists concentrated on manmade imagery, especially machines and the industrial landscape. These subjects were presented in crisp, hard-edged clarity. While some artists, including Stuart Davis and Charles Demuth, developed GEOMETRIC styles directly influenced by CUBISM, others, including Charles Sheeler (Figure 125), stressed more NATURALISTIC aspects of the interplay of crisp form and pattern in their subjects.

primary color a hue which cannot be created at its highest intensity by mixing other colors. The primary colors are the essential elements in building a palette with which to mix other colors. Systems have been built with any number of primaries, but the most common are:

SUBTRACTIVE: red, yellow, and blue. These are the preschool primaries with which most of us had our first color experiences through tempera paints and fingerpaints.

ADDITIVE: red, green, and blue. These are the hues used by a TV set or computer monitor (RGB) to create full-color images. They are also the basic colors used in theatrical lighting.

PROCESS: cyan, magenta, and yellow. These are the transparent inks used in simple printing to create full-color images.

primitive art the art of non-Western, nontechnological societies. The term is used most frequently to describe the native tribal arts of Africa, Oceania, and the Americas. In CONTENT and STYLE, primitive art is expressive of group or societal concerns and is often an integral part of ritual and religious practice. The aesthetic concerns of primitive art exist within strictly defined, formal parameters, and the works are generally highly stylized.

The artists of primitive societies are highly trained and work to ensure continuance of their cultures' visual traditions. These traditions were developed over hundreds of years before the cultural influx from the Western world.

While primitive art does share characteristics with FOLK ART, it should not be confused with NAIVE ART.

primitivism the use of PRIMITIVE or tribal art as a model for formal innovation, particularly the expressive DISTORTION of FORM. The admiration of primitive art and the reference to its stylizations is consistent with the tendency of modern artists to look outside the established traditions of the fine arts in Western culture for sources rich in decorative or expressive potential.

printmaking reproductive image-making techniques. Printmaking media are often divided into three categories: INTAGLIO, PLANOGRAPHIC, and RELIEF. Printmaking is distinguished from other approaches to art making by the act of transferring images from a plate or stencil to their final surface. Printmaking media lend themselves to multiple reproductions of single images, but prints may also be unique, one-of-a-kind images.

process the act of producing. Throughout the course of MODERN ART, the process of creating has been emphasized as a time of continuous decision making and deliberation. Interaction with the media as the piece is being made permits new possibilities and actions which will directly affect the appearance of the finished work. Rather than allowing the process of making to be limited to the straightforward illustration of a preconceived idea, an emphasis on process fosters spontaneity and "controlled accident," allowing the inherent properties of the medium, such as the fluidity of watercolor, or the softness of pastel, to offer new FORMAL possibilities.

Vera Klement's concern with process makes her paintings documents of their formal evolution, of their coming into being. Beginning with a THUMBNAIL SKETCH (Figure 126), she allows her interaction with

FIGURE 126 Vera Klement, sketchbook
page (untitled), 1986, 5¾ × 8½".
Courtesy of the artist.

the medium, a malleable ENCAUSTIC, to guide the development of the image as it is transferred to canvas, bringing two separate major elements into an aesthetic balance (Figure 127).

process color inks and paints used in commercial printing. Process color refers to the transparent colors *cyan*, *magenta*, and *yellow*, often overprinted with black in much color printing and silkscreen. In this form of printing, a full-color image is photographically separated into discrete images which are printed one on top of another, yielding the finished image. (See also *primary color*.)

FIGURE 127 Vera Klement, *Between Door
and Distance*, 1987, oil and wax on
canvas, 6 × 9′. Courtesy of the artist.

proportion   the relationship in scale between one element and another, or between a whole and one of its parts. Proportion refers not to absolute size or amount, but to the comparison of dimensions. In OBJECTIVE DRAWING emphasis is placed on establishing correct proportional relationships between the parts of objects and between the objects represented. When transferring a scene to two dimensions, an artist often holds a pencil up in front of the scene to measure relative size and angles within it.

Intentional violation of actual proportional relationships is often employed by artists for expressive reasons. Alice Neel's portraits (Figure 6), are noted for their vitality and are distinctive in the way their proportional relationships are manipulated. (See *distortion*.)

push and pull   a phrase used to describe the paintings of Hans Hofmann, one of the most influential painters and teachers of ABSTRACT EXPRESSIONISM. "Push and pull" describes the spatial interaction of color and the sensation of colors expanding and contracting, advancing and receding, providing a dynamic tension not only upon the PICTURE PLANE, but immediately in front of and behind it as well (Figure 128 and front cover).

quadratic harmony   a color harmony based on the interrelationship of four hues equidistant from one another on the circumference of the COLOR WHEEL. Quadratic harmonies can be formed by inscribing a square over the color wheel.

FIGURE 128 Hans Hofmann, *Conjuntis Viribus*, 1963, oil on canvas, 72 × 60″. Courtesy Richard Gray Gallery, Chicago.

radial symmetry SYMMETRY around a point. Images with radial symmetry have a strong central FOCAL POINT. BILATERAL SYMMETRY exists across any AXIS drawn through the FOCAL POINT (Figure 129).

FIGURE 129 Thomas Johnston, *White Cross*, 1977, aquatint, 8 × 8″. Courtesy Francine Seders Gallery, Seattle.

Realism a movement originating in France during the mid-nineteenth century which stressed subject matter representative of its own particular time. Realist artists struggled against academic conventions to present an objective view of their daily lives. Scenes of commonplace activities were offered without the idealization or sentimentalism characteristic of mainstream art of the time.

The rallying call of the movement, "to be true to one's own time," led artists to a new range of subject matter. Believing that art should be based only on what could be seen in the course of everyday life, the Realists rejected literature, history, and religion as appropriate subject matter. This resulted in imagery as diverse as Gustave Courbet's shabby peasant workers and Edouard Manet's fashionable young Parisians. The Realist insistence on a straightforward representation of the visible world served as a foundation for the IMPRESSIONISTS, who went beyond Realism in a concerted effort to depict not only what was seen, but also the instantaneous sense of that vision.

The tenets of Realism continue to have an impact on the visual arts. Thomas Eakins's *The Gross Clinic* (Figure 130) was originally rejected from an exhibition because the subject matter, an operation in progress, was repellent in its objective rendering of blood and open flesh. The audience of the time failed to respond to the more important aspect of the painting, the calm and deliberate demeanor of Dr. Gross explaining his procedure.

FIGURE 130 Thomas Eakins, *The Gross Clinic*, 1875, oil on canvas, 96 × 78". From the Jefferson Medical College of Thomas Jefferson University, Philadelphia.

FIGURE 131 Karl Moehl, *Mike IX (Adventurer)*, 1978, acrylic on canvas, 42 × 30″. Courtesy of the artist.

A major consideration of some Realists was to reveal the worthiness of real people. They believed that the artist can alert us to sincerity and dignity in the activities of daily life. These considerations are evident in works by such contemporary artists as Karl Moehl (Figure 131), who, in an informal portrait of a college student, suggests an optimism and determination characteristic of youth.

Regionalism an art movement of the 1930s which focused on rural scenes and subjects as a means of extolling the cultural attitudes and values of ordinary Americans. Regionalist artists including Thomas Hart

FIGURE 132 Thomas Hart Benton,
Arkansas Evening, n. d., lithograph, 10⅛
× 13″. Krannert Art Museum, University
of Illinois, Urbana-Champaign.

Benton (Figure 132), John Stuart Curry, and Grant Wood (Figure 28) worked with REPRESENTATIONAL imagery and shunned the abstract stylistic developments which were a part of European Modernism at that time.

relief PRINTMAKING techniques in which the parts of the image not to be printed are carved or etched away from the plate, leaving the raised area to be printed. Common relief printmaking techniques include linoleum block prints, WOODCUT, and WOOD ENGRAVING.

repetition multiple occurrence. Repetition is a fundamental unifying factor in works of art. Any of the FORMAL ELEMENTS may be repeated in an image.

Repetition may be obvious, with clearly discernible patterns and rhythm such as that found in the work of Roger Brown (Figure 13), or it may be more subtle, as in the work of Hans Hofmann (Figure 128 and front cover), which uses repetition of similar shapes, textures, and colors.

representational having the quality of resemblance. Representational art is made up of imagery which is intended to bear a visual resemblance, however ABSTRACT, to an external world. Representational art may be highly abstract, as in de Kooning's *Woman II* (Figure 7); NATURALISTIC, as in James Winn's landscape (Figure 133); or depict imaginary imagery, as in

FIGURE 133 James Winn, *Clearing*, 1985, acrylic on paper, 30 × 72″. Courtesy of Struve Gallery, Chicago.

FIGURE 134 David Klamen, *Untitled*, 1985, oil on canvas, 4 × 8'. Courtesy of Marianne Deson Gallery.

FIGURE 135 Susanne Slavick, *Pulse*, 1983, oil on canvas, 84 × 60″. Courtesy of Struve Gallery, Chicago.

David Klamen's painting (Figure 134). Representational art is the opposite of NONOBJECTIVE art.

resist in ETCHING, a material impervious to acid. Resist is used to protect areas of the plate from being etched. Common resists include asphaltum, beeswax, and rosin.

rhythm regular repetition. In art, rhythm results from the perception of intervals between repeated elements or gestures in an image. Rhythms may be described as regular, flowing, progressive, alternating, syncopated, or a combination of the above. Susanne Slavick employs a variety of rhythms in her painting *Pulse* (Figure 135). The interactions among the progressive rhythm of the radiating waves, the regular rhythm of the trees, and the syncopated rhythm of the white billows of smoke are a major source of animation in the painting.

saturation see *intensity*

scale the relative, perceived, or experienced size of an image or object.

FIGURE 136 William Wiley, *Wizdumb Bridge*, 1969, watercolor on paper, 24 × 30″. Courtesy of Struve Gallery, Chicago.

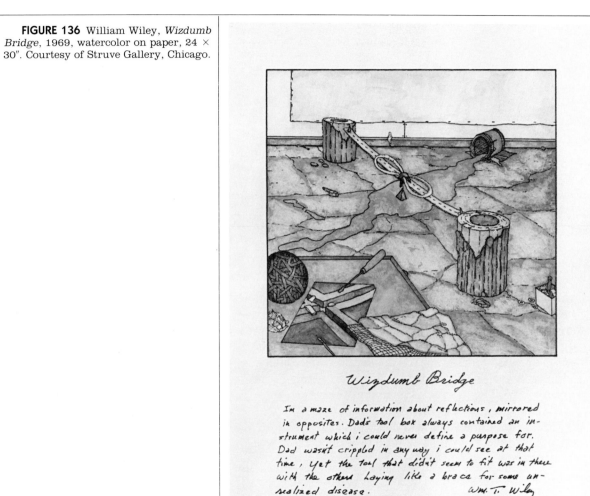

school in art a school refers to a group of artists whose work springs from a common body of thought and shares certain characteristics. For example, the 1950s New York School was bound together by shared concepts of the importance of formal concerns in artmaking and by the expression of those concepts.

script hand-written text. The use of script as opposed to TYPE to present TEXT in an image conveys a sense of the presence of the artist and of the uniqueness of the object. William Wiley frequently incorporates script in his images. In *Wizdumb Bridge* (Figure 136), an informal, almost conversational quality is evoked by the handwritten caption. The intimacy conveyed by the immediacy of the artist's handwriting provides a window into his life and mind.

In addition to serving as a title or description, as it does in the Wiley or in the work of Hollis Sigler (see Figure 158), script may also be integrated throughout an image, labeling and providing commentary, as in the work of Reverend Howard Finster (see Figure 168).

secondary color a HUE which results from mixing two PRIMARIES. Secondary colors are found midway between the primaries on the circumference of the COLOR WHEEL (Figure 137).

semiotics the study of SIGNS, SYMBOLS, and symbolism. Semiotics has its roots in philosophy—specifically in linguistics, the study of the origin of and location of meaning within language. Semiotics draws a distinction between signs and symbols, and what they represent. Semiotics explains CONTENT and meaning in terms of the relationships between "signifiers" and the concepts to which they refer.

serigraphy see *silkscreen*

shade a color of lower value made by mixing the color with black. (See also *tone*.)

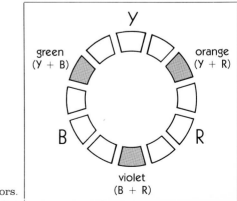

FIGURE 137 Secondary colors.

FIGURE 138 Types of shapes.

shape a closed CONTOUR. Shape is understood in terms of its perimeter or outline. Shapes are characterized in a variety of ways and derive their character from the interrelationships of parts of their contours (Figure 138).

shared contour an intentional violation of the conventions of OVERLAPPING. Shared contour is achieved by placing spatially separated objects in such a way that their contours align visually. This suggests that they are adjacent to one another and flattens and distorts the PICTORIAL SPACE. Gaylen Hansen (Figure 139) makes active use of shared contour to create multiple ambiguities in his work. Note for example how the tail of the dog fits into the row of fenceposts and how the wing of the bird aligns with the profile of the figure.

sign a graphic pattern or image which conveys a specific message. (See also *semiotics*.)

silkscreen a PRINTMAKING process in which colored inks are forced through a fine fabric mesh. The areas to be printed are controlled by blocking out the sections of the mesh which are not intended to print. Silkscreen lends itself to the reproduction of broad, flat areas of color.

silverpoint a drawing technique in which marks are made by rubbing a soft, nonferrous metal, usually silver, on a GESSO or similar GROUND. In silverpoint, the metal is the PIGMENT, and it is deposited directly on the ground, with no MEDIUM. The mark-making process is the same as dragging a coin on a painted wall.

FIGURE 139 Gaylen Hansen, *Kernel in the Farmyard*, 1974, acrylic on canvas, 36½ × 49″. Private Collection.

Silverpoint produces a delicate, semitransparent mark which evolves in time as the metal oxidizes. As a silverpoint drawing "matures," the line assumes the richness and range of color of tarnished silver.

While silver is the metal most often used, silverpoint can be made with any relatively soft metal which can be abraded by the ground.

simultaneous contrast a phenomenon of PERCEIVED COLOR. When a relatively small area of one color is presented against a field of another color, our perception of the smaller area of color is altered in response to the relationship between the two colors.

Simultaneous-contrast effects were first discussed at the end of the nineteenth century by the French color theorist Michel Chevreul, a chemist specializing in dyes for textiles. He noticed that the perceived color of the threads in tapestries changed depending on the colors of the surrounding areas.

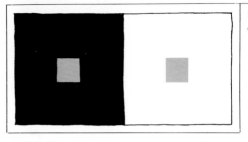

FIGURE 140 Example of simultaneous contrast of value.

The mind may be understood as a kind of image-enhancement device. It focuses its attention on the figure in FIGURE/GROUND relationships. To aid in this focusing of attention, the mind enhances the contrasts between figure and ground by seeking out differences and exaggerating them. For example, when viewing a gray dot against a black or white background (Figure 140), the mind seizes on the contrast in VALUE and magnifies it. Against the low-value background, the gray is perceived as higher in value (lighter) than when it is seen against the high-value background.

In its effort to enhance contrast, the mind seizes on whatever contrast is available between two visual events. Just as a neutral grey will be perceived as higher or lower in value depending on its context, HUE and INTENSITY are also tempered by context. When two colors interact, the mind seeks to increase the contrast between them. It is for this reason that COMPLEMENTARY hues seems to "vibrate" when juxtaposed. The COLOR WHEEL shows that the two hues are already as far apart as possible and that it is not possible to increase the contrast between them.

The importance of simultaneous contrast to the artist is that color decisions cannot be made independent of context. Specific decisions, especially regarding value, must be made by viewing proposed color in its intended surroundings.

sketch a drawing made in support of a finished work. Sketches are preparatory drawings. They may be made before work is begun on a piece or while it is in progress. Sketches aid in and elucidate the design process. The purpose of a sketch may be to record a new idea, to explore possible compositions, to resolve difficulties with one or another of the details of an image, or simply to provide an outlet for visual ramblings and musings.

Sketches are often incomplete. They may also be accompanied by written notes. Sketches convey a sense of possibility revealed, of thought in action. They may be distinguished from finished works by their apparent casualness (Figures 141 and 141a).

While we generally associate art and design with finished products, it is important to realize the essential role that sketches play in the design process. Failings in finished works can often be attributed to a failure to sketch adequately, rather than to a lack of ability on the part of the artist or designer.

FIGURE 141 Pablo Picasso, *Sans Titre* [Untitled], 1898, conté crayon and ink on paper, 12½ × 9½″ (two sides.) Courtesy of Richard Gray Gallery.

FIGURE 141a

125

sketchbook a bound book of blank paper used for the development of ideas, the recording of thoughts, the taking of notes, doodling, and drawing. A sketchbook is a tangible and visible record of the mental process. Its primary importance is as a chronicle of the evolution of an artist's work.

A sketchbook can be useful to the artist long after it is completed. Retrospective examination of where one has been can yield insight into where one is and where one's work may be leading. It is striking how often the major themes of an artist's mature work can be discerned in early sketchbooks.

There is nothing inappropriate for inclusion in a sketchbook. As a visual journal, the sketchbook is in many ways the most important artifact created by the student or mature artist.

Social Realism a human-centered art which addresses the political and social situations of its time. Social Realism is directed toward a mass audience. Its messages and concerns are not elitist. The stylistic tendencies of Social Realist painters are characterized by a generalized realism and a rejection of ABSTRACT tendencies in so far as they detract from the legibility of the imagery and its message.

Social Realism has traditionally been associated with the political left. Its history is primarily identified with the Mexican mural movement and art produced under the Works Progress Administration of the depression era. It has centered on controversies and problems affecting the poor and socially disadvantaged. Artists associated with American Social Real-

FIGURE 142 Burichenko, *Warning*, 1985, oil on canvas, 79¾ × 57¾″. Courtesy of Struve Gallery, Chicago.

ism include Ben Shahn, Philip Evergood, and the muralist Diego Rivera.

In totalitarian states such as the Soviet Union, Social Realism has become the official government style. Rather than being an expression of conflict or protest, Social Realism in this context is used as a vehicle to assert common goals and accomplishments. Burichenko's *Warning* (Figure 142) exalts the heroism of the Russian soldier in the service of his country. (See also *topical*.)

spatial color   the use of color to enhance an illusion of space or depth. It is commonly thought that color has spatial qualities. WARM, opaque, and high-INTENSITY colors are seen as advancing toward the viewer, while COOL, transparent, and low-intensity colors are seen

as receding into the PICTURE PLANE. (See front cover and *push and pull*.)

split-complementary harmony   a color relationship in which a dominant HUE is balanced by colors found on both sides of its true COMPLEMENT on the circumference of the COLOR WHEEL. For example, a split-complementary harmony could be built around yellow by balancing it with blue-purple and red-purple (Figure 143).

stencil   a thin sheet of material from which an image to be produced is cut. The negative (open) area of the stencil usually, but not always, translates as POSITIVE SHAPE in the created picture.

The stenciling process can be used to encourage an impersonal sense of making pictures. Patrick Siler

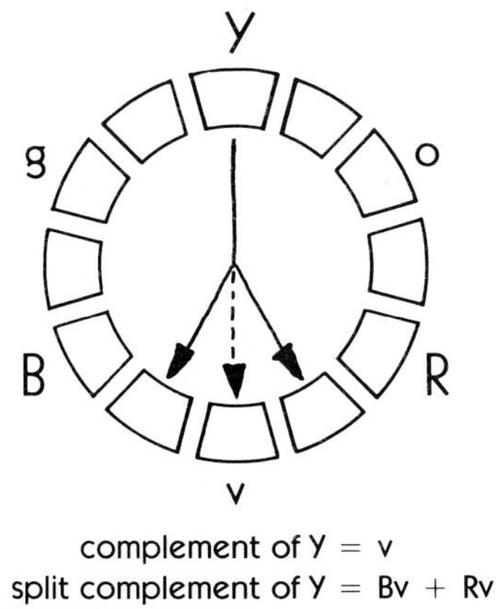

complement of Y = v
split complement of Y = Bv + Rv

Hue	Complement	Split-complement
YELLOW	violet	RED-violet BLUE-violet
orange	BLUE	BLUE-violet BLUE-green
RED	green	BLUE-green YELLOW-green
violet	YELLOW	YELLOW-green YELLOW-orange
BLUE	orange	YELLOW-orange RED-orange
green	RED	RED-orange RED-violet

FIGURE 143 Split-complementary harmonies.

(Figure 144) uses crudely cut stencils to give vitality to his work. Additionally, stencils are a means of allowing artists to readily reproduce an image or set of images across a BODY OF WORK.

Stencils are often used with AIRBRUSH and in SILK-SCREEN.

FIGURE 144 Patrick Siler, *Death and Radio #2*, 1982, acrylic on canvas, 29 × 29″. Courtesy of Linda Farris Gallery, Seattle.

Stijl, de a Dutch art movement founded in 1917, which extended CUBIST concerns for geometry and measured space. De Stijl painters, including Piet Mondrian and Theo van Doesberg, began working with NATURALISTIC imagery but simplified and reduced their canvases to GEOMETRIC abstractions based on the dynamic interplay of asymmetrically placed rectilinear units of unmodulated color. Mondrian sought a harmony in his compositions which would echo the underlying harmonies he sensed in nature (Figure 145).

The de Stijl artists envisioned widespread applications for their reductivist aesthetic, and sculptors, architects, and designers became active with the group. The movement collapsed with the advent of World War II, but its aesthetics have had a continuing impact on the visual arts, especially graphic design and architecture.

FIGURE 145 Piet Mondrian, *Composition*, 1922, oil on canvas, 21¾ × 21⅛″. Courtesy of the Menil Collection, Houston.

FIGURE 146 Robert DeVoe, *Still Life with Red and Green Tomatoes*, 1984, watercolor on paper, 25 × 37¾". Courtesy of Struve Gallery, Chicago.

still life a painting or drawing based on a grouping of inanimate objects. A still life may be a purely FORMAL study, or it may make symbolic or ALLEGORICAL references. The degree of NATURALISM in still life can vary from the careful rendering of Robert Devoe (Figure 146) to the bold abstraction of Roy Lichtenstein (Figure 147).

study a sketch, drawing, or painting made to explore details of FORM or COMPOSITION in preparation for a finished piece. Compositional studies, such as Vera Klement's THUMBNAIL SKETCH (Figure 126), omit the detail of the finished piece, while detail studies (Figure 4) focus on specific elements of the finished piece. Studies can convey a sense of informality, fresh-

FIGURE 147 Roy Lichtenstein, *Still Life with Attache Case*, 1976, oil and magna on canvas. Courtesy of Richard Gray Gallery. Photo by Bevan Davies.

ness, and daring which may be lacking in a finished work, and they may provide insight into the artist's decision-making process.

style a distinctive manner of visual expression in which the FORMAL ELEMENTS of a work of art are combined in such a way as to give a consistent visual expression to the work.

The term *style* has a broad range of applications. Style can refer to the interaction of the artist's touch with his or her medium, as, for example, a PAINTERLY style. *Personal style* describes the singular look of a given individual's work. As an artist matures, he or she may embrace a personal style that becomes as unique as handwriting or a signature. *Historical* or *period style* refers to the distinctive look of works of art produced within a given period of time or historical context. Picasso's "Blue Period" is an example of period style. Style also describes the appearance of works produced by a SCHOOL or by artists of a given region; for example, the style of French Impressionism.

Style refers exclusively to the visual appearance of a work of art. A particular style or set of stylistic characteristics may typify a MOVEMENT, but style alone is not enough to define a movement.

subtractive color color created by the absorbtion of light frequencies by pigments or filters. Subtractive color describes the ways in which paints are mixed or what will be seen through stacked filters of various colors. When COMPLEMENTS are mixed *subtractively*, the result is a low-INTENSITY HUE tending toward dark gray. When they are mixed ADDITIVELY they tend toward white.

Superrealism see *Photorealism*

support the surface on which a two-dimensional image is made. Common supports include CANVAS, ILLUSTRATION BOARD, and PAPER.

Suprematism a Russian movement of the late 1910s and the '20s based on a belief in the spiritual transcendence of NONOBJECTIVE forms divorced from the external world of material realities. The prime exponent of Suprematism, Kasimir Malevich, began working in a CUBIST-inspired mode but found the pictorial references to things of the natural world restrictive and incompatible with his mystical outlook. His mature works, like the works of other Suprematists, are characterized by highly simplified, nonobjective paintings based on the interplay of sharply defined rectilinear units of flat color (Figure 148).

As with CONSTRUCTIVISM, Suprematism found a sympathetic audience at the Bauhaus, where many artists were predisposed to a high degree of abstraction in painting.

surreal a strange hyper-real or "beyond the real" quality. Surreal imagery frequently conveys a dreamlike quality through meticulously represented forms juxtaposed in bizarre and unexpected ways. Surreal also describes works which provoke ambiguous, disconcerting, and unsettling feelings.

The term "surreal" is commonly used to describe works created outside of the art movement SURREALISM. While there are strong correlations between contemporary works with surreal qualities such as the paintings of Donald Roller Wilson (Figure 149), and

FIGURE 148 Kasimir Malevich, *Suprematist Composition*, 1916, oil on canvas, 18 × 13¾″. Courtesy of the Menil Collection, Houston.

FIGURE 149 Donald Roller Wilson, *Beverly Knew the Signs of Art Were Primary But She Wouldn't Tell Anyone Because She Wanted to Be the Only One to Know*, 1986, oil on linen panel, 10 × 12″. Collection of Judy and Howard Tullman. Photo Courtesy of Coe Kerr Gallery, Inc.

the works produced by the artists of the Surrealist movement, the contemporary artist working with surreal imagery does not necessarily hold the social and cultural views of the Surrealists.

Surrealism   a movement launched in Paris in 1924 by the poet André Breton, who declared his purpose to be a search for the higher reality—the "surreality"—of the subconscious mind. Greatly influenced by FREUD-IAN theory, Breton viewed the subconscious mind as the repository of the imagination, and he urged artists to bring repressed irrationalities held in the subconscious to the surface in pictorial form. Surrealism aimed to liberate the artistic imagination from complacency and subservience to middle-class values.

Two separate but interdependent types of imagery emerged in the early years of the movement. *Abstract or Calligraphic Surrealism* is characterized by the interplay of highly ABSTRACT or NONOBJECTIVE forms, frequently BIOMORPHIC in appearance, which were often generated by automatic techniques (see *automatism*) similar to those employed earlier by artists of the DADA movement. Among the artists of this branch of Surrealism are André Masson, whose works frequently convey a sense of violence, and Joan Miró, whose works are generally more fanciful and lyrical.

The *verisitic* or *illusionistic* branch of Surrealism used bizarre juxtapositions of sympathetic or visually incongruous elements, usually rendered with a clear illusionism, so that the pairing of objects would evoke a hallucinatory sense of mystery or dread. Violence and repressed sexual yearnings frequently served as subjects for these artists, and their works had tremen-dous shock value for the established tastes of the time. The paintings of Salvador Dali and Rene Magritte exemplify this branch of Surrealism.

The enigmatic paintings of Max Ernst (Figure 150) and Yves Tanguy (Figure 27) incorporate aspects of both branches of Surrealism and are indicative of the visual interplay between the two groups.

As a movement, Surrealism was largely played out by the onset of World War II, though its influence persisted after the war as the ABSTRACT EXPRESSION-ISTS continued investigations into the workings of the subconscious mind.

symbol   an image which represents something other than itself. Symbols are understood in two ways: as images in their own right, and as surrogates for that which they represent. Symbols are distinct from SIGNS in that signs have the singular purpose of conveying a message while symbols are more indirect, evoking a range of associations. Signs point; symbols represent.

Symbolism   a turn-of-the-century movement which stressed mysterious subjects and provoked complex and often unsettling emotions. Symbolism is regarded as a reaction against the NATURALISM of IMPRES-SIONISM, and its emphasis on optical sensation and accessible subject matter. Symbolism reinstituted romantic ties to literature and often evoked imaginative NARRATIVE situations. Symbolist artists including Gustave Moreau and Odilon Redon (Figure 151) developed distinctly personal styles responsive to their eccentric and highly subjective concerns.

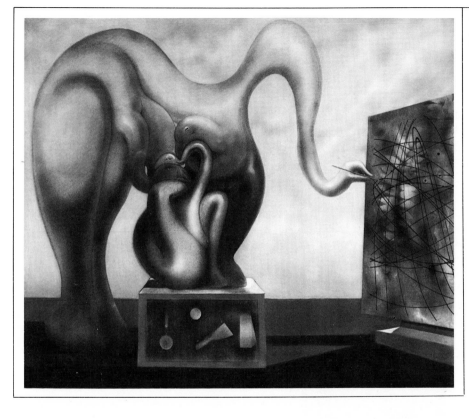

FIGURE 150 Max Ernst, *Surrealism and Painting*, 1942, oil on canvas, 77 × 92″. Courtesy of the Menil Collection, Houston.

FIGURE 151 Odilon Redon, *Silence*, 1911, oil on gesso paper, 21¼ × 21½″. Collection, The Museum of Modern Art, New York. Lillie P. Bliss Collection. Gift of Mrs. John D. Rockefeller 3rd.

symmetry the correlation between images reflected about an AXIS. Common forms of symmetry include BILATERAL SYMMETRY and RADIAL SYMMETRY.

synaesthesia literally, the confusion or substitution of one sense for another. In art the term is used metaphorically to describe such effects as a color so vibrant and rich that it "resounds." The concept held particularly strong significance for the Russian painter Wasily Kandinsky, one of the first NONOBJECTIVE painters.

tempera a water-mixable paint made by suspending pigment in an emulsion of egg yolk and water. Tempera colors are generally transparent, dry quickly, and do not blend well. They are therefore often applied in a linear manner, using hatching to develop depth and transitions from one color to another.

POSTER PAINTS are often called tempera.

tension a term used to describe situations or structures which seem in flux or unresolved. Tension arises in situations where something is sensed as being "about

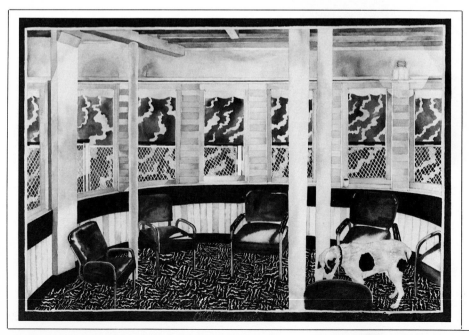

FIGURE 152 Linda Okazaki, *Old Friends*, 1984, watercolor, 40 × 60″. Courtesy of Francine Seders Gallery, Seattle. Photo by Chris Eden.

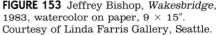
FIGURE 153 Jeffrey Bishop, *Wakesbridge*, 1983, watercolor on paper, 9 × 15″. Courtesy of Linda Farris Gallery, Seattle.

to happen." It is important not to confuse tension with agitation or chaos. Tension is present in the quiet *before* the storm and is introduced in a structure when the structure is placed under stress. If the structure succumbs to the pressure, the tension is relieved.

In art and design, tension results from a dynamic opposition of FORMAL ELEMENTS suggesting unresolved relationships or events about to happen. Tension can be introduced by contrasts of COLOR, as in PUSH AND PULL; FIGURE/GROUND ambiguities; or the dynamics of composition, as in *Old Friends* by Linda Okazaki (Figure 152), where the placement of

the dog at the right side of the image, separated from the rest of the room by the vertical pillars, offers a contrast to the openness of the space at the left. Additional tension is introduced through the varieties of pattern and abrupt shifts in value.

Tension is often felt *between* two elements, especially when they are almost touching one another. For example, Jeffrey Bishop uses the broken contour of the geometric elements to create a dynamic tension across the central vertical AXIS of his painting *Wakesbridge* (Figure 153).

Psychological tension can also be introduced into an image by creating unresolved NARRATIVE situations.

tertiary color a HUE which is the result of mixing a SECONDARY COLOR with an adjacent PRIMARY; it is found between the two of them on the COLOR WHEEL (Figure 154).

Some color-mixing systems refer to HUES of moderate intensities (Figure 155) as tertiaries.

text words. When words become an active part of a piece of visual art, our relationship to the art object is very different than when we are confronted with only FORMAL information. The introduction of text into an image activates a different kind of understanding on the part of the viewer. While we can stand before a

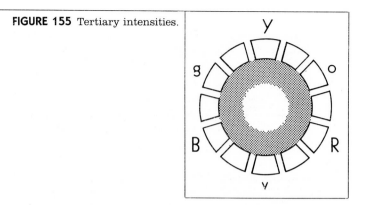

FIGURE 155 Tertiary intensities.

painting and passively allow the image to "wash over" us, an image with text in it requires action—reading.

The act of reading affects the understanding of works of art in a variety of ways. Reading is linear—words are read in order. The mind does not wander around in a paragraph in the same way it can in a landscape. Additionally, reading generally implies an intermediate translation of letters to words and words to images, while a painting or drawing may be understood immediately. Finally, recent research in the workings of the brain suggests that reading, the interpretation of words, is an activity of the left hemisphere of the brain; while the interpretation of spatial relationships, looking at images, is an activity of the brain's right hemisphere.

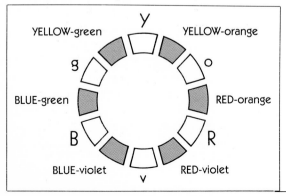

FIGURE 154 Tertiary hues.

Since CUBISM, modern artists have explored the use of text in their work in varying degrees. Occasionally, words may function as SIGNS or SYMBOLS. Standing alone, a word may be recognized immediately and evoke a range of associations. This is the case in McDermott and McGough's painting *Queer—1885* (Figure 38). At other times, words may appear as part of complex images, providing formal variety and adding an opportunity for a secondary level of revelation and meaning, as in collages using bits of printed matter (Figure 40). Another way in which words can be used is to label or name the objects or images depicted, as in Figure 156.

FIGURE 156 Robert Rauschenberg, *Sky Garden*, 1969, lithograph and silkscreen, 89 × 37⅝″. Krannert Art Museum, University of Illinois, Urbana-Champaign.

Text becomes a dominant force when it is the primary vehicle for the meaning of an image. This is the case in Magritte's painting (Figure 157). This piece, an image of a pipe labeled "this is not a pipe," and titled "The Treason of Images" speaks explicitly about issues of representation. (See also *script; semiotics; type*.)

texture tactile surface. In art and design, texture may be physical, as in IMPASTO, or it may be purely visual. Visual textures result from the creation of a field of marks small enough, close together enough, and in sufficient quantity that we relate to them as a pattern, a visual whole. Visual texture may mimic external reality with TROMPE L'OEIL effects, or it may be more ABSTRACT.

Hollis Sigler's explicit brushwork endows her painting (Figure 158) with a strong physical as well as visual texture, creating a tangible tactile presence.

FIGURE 157 Rene Magritte, *La Trahison des images (Ceci n'est pas une pipe)* [The Treason of Images (This is not a pipe)], 1928-1929, oil on canvas, 23⅝ × 37". Los Angeles County Museum of Art. Purchased with Funds Provided by the Mr. and Mrs. William Preston Harrison Collection.

FIGURE 158 Hollis Sigler, *She Has Secrets Even from Herself*, 1986, oil on board, 12 × 15″. Courtesy of Dart Gallery and Elmhurst College Library.

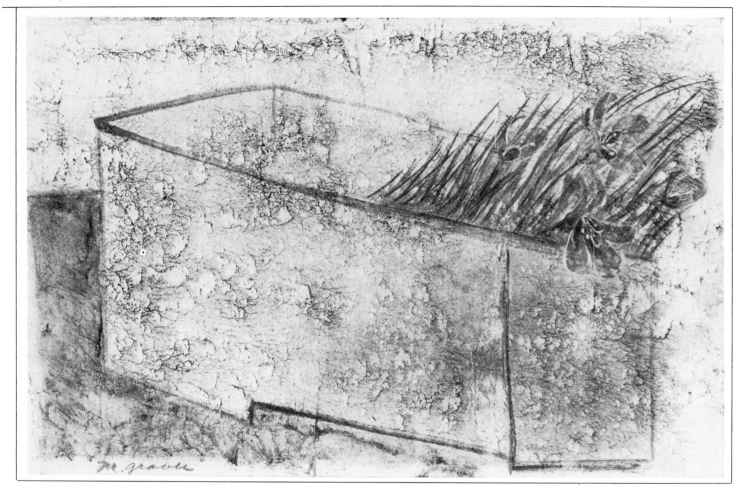

FIGURE 159 Morris Graves, *Box of Flowers*, 1950, mixed media on paper, 8⅛ × 12⅞″. Private Collection.

Morris Graves creates a range of purely visual textures in his STILL LIFE (Figure 159).

three-point perspective   a form of LINEAR PERSPECTIVE used to represent scenes from an exaggerated point of view. In three-point perspective vertical lines as well as horizontal lines recede to vanishing points (Figure 160). Three-point perspective is often used to present a BIRD'S-EYE or WORM'S-EYE VIEW.

thumbnail sketch   a very small sketch with little or no detail. Thumbnail sketches aid in the visualization of COMPOSITION and VALUE relationships (Figure 126).

tint   a color mixed with white. When a paint is mixed with white, its VALUE is raised, creating a tint. This mixed color will generally have a lower INTENSITY than pure color.

tinting strength   a measure of the extent to which a paint maintains its INTENSITY when mixed with white, with higher strength attributed to those paints which best maintain their intensity. Tinting strength varies depending on the PIGMENT used in the formulation of the paint.

tone   a lower-INTENSITY color made by mixing a HUE with its COMPLEMENT. Tones are usually of lower VALUE than the base hue and are often considered richer than SHADES because of the use of the complement.

Tones bridge the gap between complementary hues, reducing the extremity of contrast and unifying images built around a complementary harmony.

Some color-mixing systems consider mixtures of a hue with black to be tones. Such a mixture yields results similar to the mixture of a hue with its complement, but at a lower value.

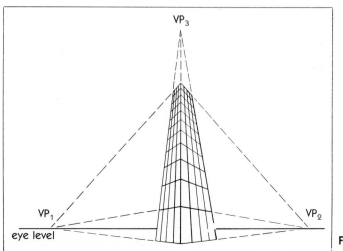

FIGURE 160 Three-point perspective.

FIGURE 161 Leon Golub, *White Squad*
(III), 1982, acrylic on canvas, 120 × 172″.
Courtesy of Barbara Gladstone Gallery,
New York. Photo by David Reynolds.

FIGURE 162 Don Lake, *Object of*
Affection, 1977, transparent watercolor,
26¾ × 17⅛″. Courtesy of the artist.

FIGURE 163 John Marin, *Lower Manhattan*, 1920, watercolor, 21⅞ × 26¾″. Collections, The Museum of Modern Art, New York. The Philip L. Goodwin Collection.

topical having content which refers to specific contemporary social or political events. Leon Golub (Figure 161) uses his art to make forceful statements about political and human rights issues.

transparent watercolor a water-thinned painting material which is applied in a transparent WASH over a white paper ground. Transparent watercolor relies on the white of the ground for high VALUES.

Watercolor can be handled in a variety of ways. In Don Lake's *Object of Affection* (Figure 162), the MEDIUM is carefully built up in layers so that the metallic surfaces of the machinery are clearly evoked through the smooth sensation of flat color. John Marin (Figure 163) used a more fluid and EXPRESSIONISTIC GESTURE, maintaining our awareness of the surface of the paper as a key element in the work.

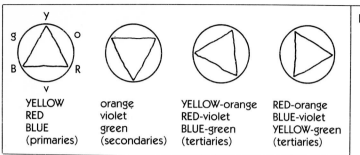

FIGURE 164 Triadic harmonies.

triadic harmony a color harmony based on the inter-relationship of three hues equidistant from one another on the circumference of the COLOR WHEEL. The PRIMARY COLORS form a triadic harmony as do the SECONDARY COLORS. Additional triadic harmonies can be found by inscribing an equilateral triangle over the color wheel (Figure 164).

triptych a work of art composed of three adjacent but independent panels or FORMATS, presented together and meant to be viewed as a single unit.

trompe l'oeil French for "trick the eye." Trompe l'oeil (pronounced "tromp-loy") painting or drawing seeks to fool the viewer into believing that the rendered image is truly there rather than merely represented. Most works of art require viewers to suspend disbelief and actively involve their imagination in order to complete the image and make it believable. Trompe l'oeil is more extreme than most REPRESENTATIONAL art in that it fools us, at least for a moment, into seeing things which are not there (Figure 165).

two-dimensional flat. Two-dimensional objects are described in terms of height and width. Their thickness is not considered significant except as texture.

two-point perspective a form of LINEAR PERSPECTIVE which is used to represent objects seen at an angle relative to the PICTURE PLANE. In two-point perspective only verticals remain parallel to the picture plane; all other lines recede to vanishing points (Figure 166).

type uniform letters usually formed mechanically. Type is distinguished from SCRIPT by its unvarying adherence to prescribed formal limits. It can give textual information an anonymous and authoritative feeling. Type is the medium manipulated by typographic artists (see Figure 156).

unity the quality of oneness. Most AESTHETIC theories refer to unity in concert with VARIETY as a distinguishing characteristic of works of art. Unity results from the consistent application of design principles, singular vision on the part of the artist, REPETITION,

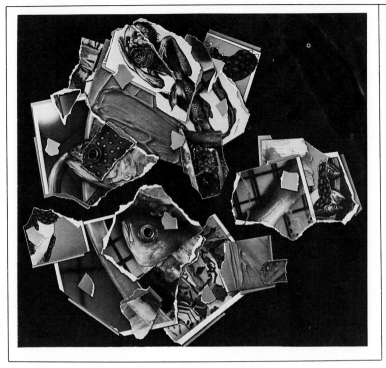

FIGURE 165 Richard Heipp, *Synthetic Collage III, Recipe Series III*, 1984-1985, acrylic on plastic, shaped triptych, 96 × 96". Courtesy Francine Seders Gallery, Seattle. Photo by Larry Dixon.

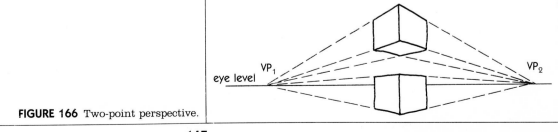

FIGURE 166 Two-point perspective.

and HARMONY within an image. Unity must be balanced with variety to create an image with more than passing interest.

value the dimension of color which describes its lightness or darkness. Value is responsive to the reflectivity of a color. It may be understood as the relative lightness or darkness of a color when seen on a black-and-white television or in a black-and-white photograph. The closer a color's value is to white, the higher its value. The closer its value is to black, the lower the value. High value is light. Low value is dark.

Value is one of the most important visual elements in the organization of an image. The richness of expression in ACHROMATIC media such as black-and-white photography and graphite attests to the expressive power of value. A quick look at the illustrations in this book points out the attention paid to value by artists working with color as well. Although all of the reproductions are in black and white, they manage to convey an enormous amount of information about the full-color originals.

Attention to value is an acquired skill. This can be seen by comparing black-and-white snapshots to fine photography. One of the things which distinguishes amateur from professional work in photography and other media is the greater sensitivity to value on the part of the trained artist.

The importance of attention to value was further demonstrated in the TV coverage of the 1960 presidential election. The designer of the national election map for one of the major networks had developed a color-coding system to inform the viewers of the graphic flow of the returns as they came in. As one might expect, the colors used in the design contrasted strongly in HUE, but the designer neglected to compare their values. Those watching the election returns on black-and-white televisions saw nothing but a uniform gray.

value scale a chart showing even steps in VALUE from white to black. MUNSELL quantified value on a scale from 0 to 10, with 0 representing black and 10 representing white (Figure 167).

FIGURE 167 Value scale.

vanishing point in LINEAR PERSPECTIVE, a point, on or off the page, where parallel lines moving away from the viewer into the PICTORIAL SPACE converge. (See also *one-point perspective*; *two-point perspective*; *three-point perspective*.)

variations a series of pieces or images, similar to one another in most major respects, with a limited range of elements changed from one piece or image to the next. In looking at a group of variations, we are always aware of the theme they have in common. A major source of interest may be the observation of the varied effects of the minor changes.

A series of variations is distinguished by how much they have in common with one another, not how different they are.

variety difference. Variety is needed in works of art to balance those factors creating UNITY. Variety results from the use of unexpected and contrasting visual and conceptual elements. These elements provide variety because of the differences between them and the dominant visual structure. It is necessary to understand the unifying GESTALT of an image in order to appreciate the role of the contrasting elements which create variety.

visionary art art made in response to an individual, often spiritual, vision. Visionary art may have religious or utopian themes and is often created by NAIVE artists like the Reverend Howard Finster (Figure 168).

FIGURE 168 Reverend Howard Finster, *City of Mosola (Pearl Granet)*, 1986, enamel on wood, 33½ × 29½". Courtesy of the Phyllis Kind Gallery—Chicago/New York. Photo by William H. Bengtson.

volume color the PERCEIVED COLOR of a semitransparent volume. The perceived color of a deep river or a glass of iced tea is altered by the passage of light through the liquid.

warm color a color whose HUE is in the area from red to yellow on the COLOR WHEEL (Figure 169). Warm colors tend to advance visually.

wash a transparent area of pigment covering a broad area of an image.

watercolor a water-soluble paint in which the BINDER is gum arabic, glycerine, and/or honey. (See also *gouache*; *transparent watercolor*.)

woodcut a RELIEF printmaking technique in which the image to be printed is carved into the surface grain of a wooden plank. When a softwood is used, the grain may be visible in the finished print, contributing visual TEXTURE and sometimes PATTERN as in Figure 170.

wood engraving a RELIEF printmaking technique in which the image to be printed is created in the endgrain of a finely grained hardwood. This technique enables the production of much finer detail than does WOODCUT.

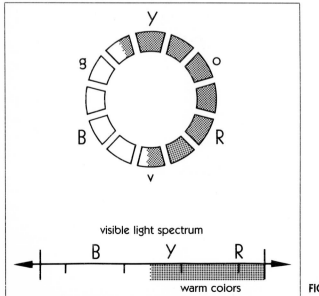

FIGURE 169 Warm colors.

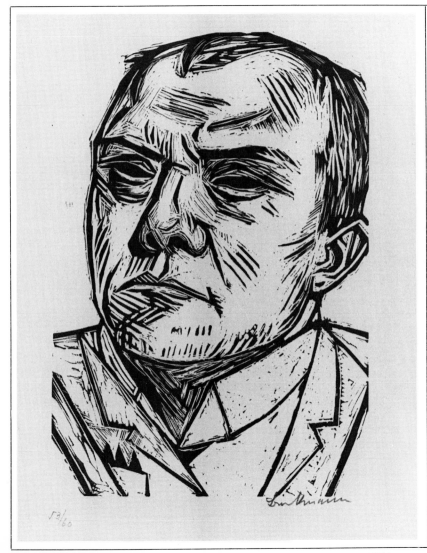

FIGURE 170 Max Beckmann, *Self Portrait*, 1922, 8⅞ × 6⅛″. Courtesy of Worthington Gallery, Chicago, IL.

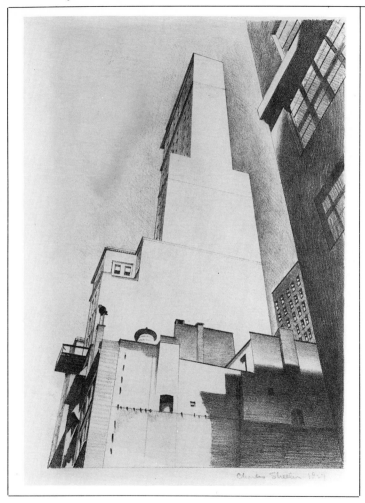

FIGURE 171 Charles Sheeler, *Delmonico Building*, 1926, lithograph, 9¾ × 6¾".
Courtesy of Associated American Artists, New York.

worm's-eye view a point of view in which the scene depicted is shown from an exaggeratedly low vantage point (Figure 171).

xerography the process of making images with photo-mechanical copying machines. With recent developments in copiers enabling them to print on a wide variety of papers and in color, artists are increasingly exploring the potential of these machines as tools for the making of both unique images and multiple editions.

3
Exercise and Analysis

The bulk of your energies in studio classes is devoted to two activities: solving problems and critiquing those solutions. In this chapter you will find generic design exercises, questions to ask about your work and that of others, and suggested strategies for class critique.

EXERCISES

1. Make a detailed OBJECTIVE drawing of an ORGANIC object using only LINE (no MODELING or VALUE gradations). The drawing should fill the entire FORMAT, with the BORDER functioning as a window. This drawing will require patience and careful observation. There should be a point-for-point correspondence between each mark on your page and a visual aspect of the object being rendered.

2. Use a CROPPING FRAME to select an interesting COMPOSITION from a small section of an image, object, or scene. The drawing created in Exercise 1 may be used as a source. Transfer this pattern, within a clearly delineated BORDER, to your FORMAT. Use pen and ink, graphite, or some other ACHROMATIC medium to MODEL various areas within the piece and create a convincing PICTORIAL SPACE.

3. Design a simple SYMBOL or SIGN to represent yourself. Your design should be composed with graphic interactions of SHAPE and should avoid reliance on LINE to define CONTOUR. Pay special attention to POSITIVE and NEGATIVE SHAPE, and FIGURE/GROUND relationships. Render the design in black (india ink, cut paper, paint, etc.) on a white ground. Your finished piece should have a broad BORDER.

4. Explore a variety of color contrasts by creating a simple STENCIL. The design from Exercise 3 may be used as a basis for the stencil. Create several dozen tiles about 1½" square in a variety of colors, seeking as wide a range of HUE, VALUE, and INTENSITY as possible. Carefully apply the chosen design in a contrasting color to each of the tiles.

Explore contrasts of hue, value, and intensity. Select a number of your tiles and arrange them in a regular GRID with a narrow space between each tile. Use some principle of COLOR interaction to organize the tiles within the grid, for example, high value at the top gradually becoming low value at the bottom. Again, be sure to leave an ample BORDER around the image.

5. Go to the library and find a reproduction of a complex painting completed before 1880 (each student should select a different image). ABSTRACT the image into a simple black-and-white VALUE pattern. View the finished works together as a class looking for similarities that may suggest structures for the organization of successful images. Sources should be limited to older historical sources in an effort to avoid abstracting already highly abstracted images. Paintings are preferred because of their reliance on large areas of value rather than LINE. Chosen images should be compositionally complex. The main concern of simple images such as portraits is more often with creating likeness than with COMPOSITION and structure.

6. Use a photocopy machine to gather images from a variety of sources, then combine them in a SURREAL COLLAGE. Pay special attention to PICTORIAL SPACE, VALUE relationships, and ATMOSPHERIC PERSPECTIVE. Endeavor to make your piece both fantastic and believable. Photocopy the finished piece and investigate the use of SPATIAL COLOR to enhance the illusion of space. (*Note:* It may be possible to photocopy the image onto a quality art paper.)

7. Explore NORMAL VALUE and the confusion of VALUE with INTENSITY by finding a full-color reproduction of a complex image containing broad areas of a range of HUES, INTENSITIES, and values. Reproduce the image ACHROMATICALLY in a full range of values, matching perfectly the value relationships in the original. Test the finished project by comparing it to the source using black-and-white TV or a black-and-white photograph. This is a very challenging exercise.

8. Experiment with the BEZOLD EFFECT by working from a CROPPED portion of a photographic image as a source. Use cyan, magenta, and yellow inks with a fine point pen to mimic PROCESS COLOR.

9. Explore the dynamics of GROUPING by creating a single image with multiple REPETITIONS of a single MOTIF in a variety of rhythms which relies upon a range of grouping devices.

10. Investigate the evocative qualities of NARRATIVE and ALLEGORICAL ART by creating a meaningful image using only NONREPRESENTATIONAL (simple GEOMETRIC and/or ORGANIC) imagery.

11. Go to the library and find a reproduction of a complex painting completed before 1880. Make a group of compositional STUDIES, paying special attention to PICTORIAL SPACE, VALUE, COLOR HARMONIES, placement of objects, and LINE OF SIGHT. Develop a COMPOSITION of your own, either REPRESENTATIONAL or NONOBJECTIVE, which shares the same underlying structure as this external source.

12. Develop an image in which the FORMAT is broken up into at least five subformats, pictures within a picture. Pay attention to the composition of each individual "frame" as well as to the page as a whole. In order to appreciate a piece, the viewer should have to attend to each individual image as well as to the whole. Possible frameworks for this exercise are the illustration of a NARRATIVE, a METAMORPHOSIS, or an activity or process. Good sources for compositional ideas include POLYPTYCHS, altarpiece paintings, instruction manuals, and action comic books.

13. Select a small portion of an enigmatic and imagery-laden

text to illustrate. One text which works very well for this project is the *I Ching or Book of Changes* (Wilhelm/Baynes, Bollingen Series XIX, Princeton University Press).

14. Establish a careful record of some event or activity over time. A detailed time log of a two-week period in an individual's life works well. Develop a "code" or "key" for transferring the information from the written record to a graphic image. You design the code, but the appearance of the finished work is determined by the record to which the code is applied. If the image is unsatisfactory, you must change the code rather than the data. The code should be applicable to a variety of records and should not immediately reveal the meaning of the finished image. The goal of this exercise is to create images which appear to be "information laden"—which will be recognized immediately as having CONTENT, even if the meaning is unclear. Good sources of ideas for the code include scientific charts and graphs, maps, demographic charts, weather maps, astrological charts, and foreign alphabets. The more personally relevant and detailed the information, the more effective the PROCESS and the finished piece.

15. Explore an idea in depth by making at least ten VARIATIONS on a response to a single challenge. The variations should be distinguished by their similarity and their focused exploration of the effect of changing a specific detail in each piece.

ANALYSIS: TWENTY QUESTIONS

The discussion of the creative process in Section 1 pointed out the key role of analysis in the cycle of creative problem-solving. It is useful to pause in your exercises, step back from your work, and critically consider your efforts. This same analysis can serve you when looking at work by your colleagues or even in museums. We present here a by-no-means conclusive list of questions to ask when analyzing a work of art.

1. What was the artist or designer trying to accomplish? How did he or she define the problem and what were his or her goals?

2. Do we as viewers break the piece down into parts for understanding? If so, how are the parts grouped—by similarity, proximity, color, material, direction, gesture, or other means? Do the groupings overlap? How?

3. Are some elements or parts of the image more important than others? Which ones?

4. Could any elements or parts of the piece be moved or deleted without drastically altering its character? If so, how many, which ones, and why?

5. If you were to do a series of variations on this piece, what form would they take? Which elements would you retain and which would you modify?

6. Are the proportional relationships within the piece appropriate? How would the piece be altered if they were changed or distorted?

7. Is the composition of the piece appropriate? How does the image relate to its format? What would it be like in a different format?

8. Is there a good balance between craftsmanship and concept? Does the quality and care of its making and materials contribute to or distract from the effectiveness of the image?

9. Is the piece surprising in any way?

10. How would your relationship with the piece change if it were turned on its side or upside down?

11. What is the smallest possible change that would significantly alter the character of the image?

12. Does the image convey a sense of control? Are there any elements in the work which appear to have been accidents? Are they successfully incorporated into the image?

13. How would the piece be changed if rendered in a different medium or at a different scale?

14. Are there any motifs in the image from other works by the artist? Do they work to the benefit or detriment of the piece?

15. Are there any aspects of the piece which remind you of the work of another artist? Do they contribute to the effectiveness of the piece?

16. To what extent does the image allow for a variety of interpretations? Does this openness dilute the strength of the work or increase its universality?

17. What would an image that was the formal or conceptual opposite of this piece look like?

18. Does the work evoke any emotional response? How?

19. Does the work suggest or reveal anything about the artist as a person or the artist's involvement in the making of the work? What?

20. Does the image have any narrative content? Does it tell a story or make a statement? What and how?

CRITIQUES: STRATEGIES AND QUESTIONS

The primary forum for communication in the school setting is the critique. It is here that the opportunity exists to see your work through the eyes of others and to share with them your perceptions of their work. Too often critiques become monologues by instructors. This can be the result of students being interested only in what the professor has to say, not realizing how much they have to offer one another.

Involving the class in critique is a continuing challenge, but it is worth the effort. One of the most important skills to be developed in foundation studio classes is the ability to speak intelligently and productively about one's work. It is essential that students learn to relate to their instructors and colleagues as collaborators and to think of their artifacts as works in progress.

One strategy that we have found effective in developing these skills involves the following elements:

- All work is hung up at the beginning of class.
- The pieces are labeled with numbers so they can be easily referred to without descriptions such as "the yellow one with the house" or "Jean's piece."
- A "theme" for the critique is presented in the form of a question.
- The students are asked to take anywhere from five to twenty minutes to write down answers to the question in their sketchbooks. In addition, the students are asked to make quick thumbnail sketches of each work presented.

At the end of this process, the critique is ready to begin. This approach yields several benefits. The numbering of pieces helps to isolate the ego of the artist from the work being discussed. The thumbnail sketches encourage the students to look carefully at every piece that has been presented. The theme question suggests a framework for looking at the images, and finally, the writing—which is not collected—ensures that each student will have something to say during the discussion which follows. In informal classes, students' conversation during this sketching and writing period often covers much of what is sought in critique.

Some possible critique themes:

1. Divide the work into two or three visual categories. Explain which category each piece belongs in and why.

2. Select the piece most similar to your own and describe their similarities and differences. Suggest relative strengths and ways in which either piece could benefit from being more like the other.

3. Invent a title for each piece and explain the appropriateness of the title.

4. On separate sheets of paper, make suggestions of ways to improve each piece. Do not write down your name. (These pieces of paper are collected and read aloud by the instructor.)

5. Vote for your favorite piece. The ballots are collected and tallied. (Usually there are clear "winners" and "losers" in this popularity contest. The work is rearranged in order of votes and students are asked to describe qualities which distinguish high vote-getters from low.)

6. Find as many visual characteristics as you can which are shared by at least three, but no more than five, of the presented pieces. (Like all of the themes, this is aimed at developing critical observation of the works presented. An effort is made to encourage the students to form innovative visual categories in which to place objects.)

7. Finished pieces are randomly assigned to each student with no student receiving his or her own work. Students are asked to present the assigned pieces as if they were filling in for a missing colleague at an important conference. They must, without consulting with the artist, explain the piece's intent, the devices used by the artist to achieve expressive goals, and the work's effectiveness. Negative comments are not permitted, but the presenter might suggest "We have considered several variations on this proposal, including . . . ."

8. You are asked to select your favorite piece. Suggest three *major* changes which might be made in the piece without diminishing its quality and describe the effects that these changes would have.

Index of Artists' Names

Arneson, Robert   53
Arp, Jean   46
Arraguin, Alfredo   85, 86

Barnes, Robert   65
Beckmann, Max   151
Benton, Thomas Hart   116
Bishop, Jeffrey   137
Boccioni, Umberto   63
Brown, Roger   16
Burichenko   126

Callagahan, Kenneth   55
Cezanne, Paul   106
Christo   50, 51
Close, Chuck   1
Conger, William   98

DeForest, Roy   76
Degas, Edgar   21
De Kooning, Elaine   48

De Kooning, Willem   11
DeVoe, Robert   130
Dubuffet, Jean   72, 89
Duchamp, Marcel   20

Eakins, Thomas   8, 114
Ehle, Michael   44, 90
Ernst, Max   135
Estes, Richard   103
Evans, Walker   19

Finster, Reverend Howard   149

George, Ray   31
Golub, Leon   144
Graves, Morris   142
Green, Art   98
Guzak, Karen   25

Hansen, Gaylen   123
Hascall, Mike   88

Hayes, Randy   32
Heipp, Richard   147
Heyman, Steven   47
Hockney, David   35, 79, 88
Hofmann, Hans   112
Holder, Ken   87
Hull, Richard   104

Johnston, Thomas   113

Keating, Andrew   42, 49
Kelly, Ellsworth   83
Kerrigan, Maurie   81
Kimler, Wesley   99
Kirchner, Ernst Ludwig   31
Klamen, David   118
Klement, Vera   111
Knight, Gwen   43, 66
Kosuth, Joseph   40
Kraut, Susan   95

Lake, Don	144	Neel, Alice	11	Sigler, Hollis	141
Lawrence, Jacob	57	Nutt, Jim	29	Siler, Patrick	128
Leger, Fernand	83			Slavick, Susanne	14, 119
Levine, Sherrie	19	Okazaki, Linda	136	Spafford, Michael	56
Lichtenstein, Roy	131			Stevovich, Andrew	30, 79
Long, Bert	29	Paillé, Louise	35	Straub, Matt	59
Luks, George	60	Paschke, Ed	62		
Lundin, Norman	13	Phillips, Tony	91		
		Picasso, Pablo	33, 45, 78, 125	Tanguy, Yves	27
MacConnel, Kim	101	Pollock, Jackson	15	Tobey, Mark	14, 31
Margritte, Rene	140				
Malevich, Kasimir	133	Rabell, Arnoldo Roche	44		
Manet, Edouard	18	Rauschenberg, Robert	139	Valerio, James	39, 84
Marc, Franz	28	Redon, Odilon	135	van de Velde, Henry	21
Marin, John	145	Rivers, Larry	71	van Hoek, Hans	3
Matisse, Henri	54, 70	Rossi, Barbara	24, 97	Vasarely, Victor	96
McDermott and McGough	34	Rothko, Mark	13	Vaughan, Keith	7, 78
Moehl, Karl	115	Salle, David	49	Warhol, Andy	105
Mondrian, Piet	129	Schlemmer, Oskar	25	Wiley, William	120
Monet, Claude	73	Seurat, Georges	92	Wilson, Donald Roller	133
Morisot, Berthe	22	Sheeler, Charles	109, 152	Winn, James	117
		Sherman, Cindy	107, 108	Wonnar, Paul	74
Nakoneczny, Michael	58	Shimomura, Roger	59	Wood, Grant	27

661